Prais

"I have _____ long admired him as a voice crying in the U.S. evangelical wilderness. His words are compelling because they come from thoughtful reflection, careful research, gritty piety, and the wisdom of a life well-lived. I commend The Disparate Ones for any reader, but especially those seeking to chart a faithful Christian path through the chaos of today's American empire."

> The Rev. Emily H. McGowin, Ph.D.
> Associate Professor of Theology
> Wheaton College

"These essays were a breath of fresh air—challenging, insightful, and full of much-needed truth. In a day filled with hot takes and over-simplified arguments, Marty offers a thoughtful and nuanced perspective on a broad range of important issues."

> Marwan Aboul-Zelof, Lead Pastor
> City Bible Church
> Beirut, Lebanon

"In a day past, Jesus differentiated to Pontius Pilate the cosmic difference between his kingdom and that of Rome: "My kingdom is not of this world." Today, as Marty makes clear, a disparate band of Jesus followers must discern between two poles embedded within a system that defines Jesus as either a community organizer or a king become the projections of our own best ideals. Marty has long wrestled with the liminal space between these two poles within our existing system. Now he has put into print what the rupture of the Kingdom of Jesus means to the questions of our day, in the systems of our own making."

> Dr Todd Littleton, Pastor
> Snow Hill Baptist Church
> Tuttle, OK

I have long appreciated Marty Duren as a conversation partner. Even when we don't agree on every point, his thought-provoking arguments lead me to better articulate my own views. This collection of essays covers everything from hot button issues of the day to the joy of buying books, with its ode to tsundoku giving reason enough to add The Disparate Ones to your library.

Amy Whitfield,
Communications Executive
Author, Lottie Moon: The Girl Who
Reached the World

THE DISPARATE ONES

Essays on Being in the World but Not of the World

MARTY DUREN

MISSIONAL PRESS
-NASHVILLE, TN-

A Missional Press book

Copyright © 2024 Martin S. Duren

This book or parts thereof may not be reproduced in any form, stored in any retrieval system, or transmitted in any form by any means—electronic, mechanical, photocopy, recording, or otherwise—without prior written permission of the publisher, except as provided by United States of America copyright law. No part of this book may be used as data for 'training' any large language model or as part of any machine learning or neural network architecture. All rights reserved.

ISBN (paperback) 978-1-7362821-8-2
ISBN (E-book) 978-1-7362821-9-9

Unless otherwise noted, scripture quotations are taken from the Christian Standard Bible®, Copyright © 2017 by Holman Bible Publishers. Used by permission. Christian Standard Bible® and CSB® are federally registered trademarks of Holman Bible Publishers.

Scripture quotations marked NRSVue are from the New Revised Standard Version Updated Edition Bible, copyright 1989, 2021 by the division of Christian Education of the National Council of the Churches of Christ in the U.S.A. Used by permission. All rights reserved.

Cover design by Taylor Creative, concept by the author. Original West Bank photo of Banksy's Flower Thrower by John Dambik, licensed by Alamy. Used by permission.

Published by Missional Press, Nashville, TN.

missionalpressbooks.com

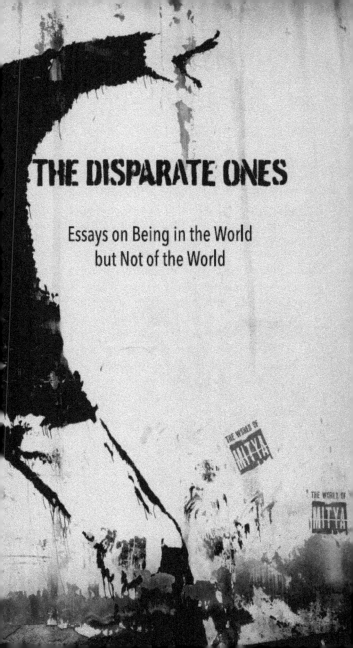

Notes

There is a longstanding conversation about footnotes and endnotes in books. Some prefer footnotes—especially in academic works—so the supplemental information is at the bottom of the same page. Others prefer endnotes so the pages are not cluttered with dividers, different fonts, etc.

This book uses endnotes. To make things easier, citations do not repeat with each new essay. So, there is only one citation each numbered [1], [2], [3], etc. The endnotes are divided by the book's chapters to assist quick lookups.

Several of these essays first appeared on Kingdom in the Midst, blog.martyduren.com. They have been edited and/or updated for this book and are identified by month and year of publication.

Acknowledgments

Nothing of substance I do is without the ongoing, patient, encouragement of my wife, Sonya. A more suitable mate God never made. Thank you for years of conversation, ideas, proofreading, corrections, and suggestions making everything I write, and my whole life, better. I love you with all my heart.

Many thanks to Sonya Duren, Dr Emily McGowin, Trey Ferguson, Dr Todd Littleton, Amy Whitfield, and Marwan Abdul-Zelof who spent valuable time reading the drafts. A special thanks to Melvin E. Edwards for also writing the forward.

All praise and thanksgiving to God the Father, Son, and Holy Spirit, from whom all blessings flow.

dis•pa•rate (dĭs´pər-ĭt, dĭ-spăr´ĭt) *adj.* ➤ Entirely distinct or different
The American Heritage Dictionary, Fifth Edition (2012 Dell Mass Market)

"But you are a chosen race, a royal priesthood, a holy nation, a people for his possession...Once you were not a people, but now you are God's people." —1 Peter 2:9, 10 *fides quaerens intellectum*

Table of Contents

Foreword   1

Essay 1 | In It, Not of It   4

Essay 2 | Torn Between Two Lovers: Christians and the U.S. Political System   12

Essay 3 | Let's Love First   22

Essay 4 | Momento Tempus. Momento Aeternum.   30

Essay 5 | A Few Thoughts about Food and Eating   38

Essay 6 | Christian Nationalism: What It Is, What It Isn't, and Why It Matters   48

Essay 7 | Tsundoku   58

Essay 8 | The Poor You Have with You Always   64

Essay 9 | Stop Saying 'Impactful'   70

Essay 10 | One Christ Follower Considers the Afghanistan Papers   74

Essay 11 | Comfortable Injustice: Christians, Race, and the U.S. Legal System   84

Essay 12 | Career and the Spirit of the Age   94

Essay 13 | The Bearable Whiteness of Being   100

Essay 14 | The American Death Penalty and the Bible   106

Essay 15 | Evangelicals in the Room Where it Happens   114

Essay 16 | Palestinians and the Limits of World Compassion   122

Essay 17 | Abortion   132

Endnotes   147

Foreword

It has been my pleasure to know Marty Duren since right before the pandemic lockdown days in early 2021. We had interacted through Twitter on a variety of subjects, and he invited to be a guest on his Uncommontary podcast to discuss my first book. It was my first time on any podcast, and I didn't know what to expect. However, even if I had known Marty better at the time, there's still no way I could have known what to expect. He can be spontaneous and sharp-witted, and sometimes leave you guessing what his next move might be. I appreciate that about him.

I found the interaction that day on his podcast to be warm and friendly. In fact, it became so friendly that we became real friends away from social media. There are few people I trust more than Marty to share a perspective with warmth and depth. Even on the rare occasion that I might disagree with him, I know his opinion is one that I need to seriously consider before dismissing. Because of that appearance on Marty's podcast, the audiobook format of my book pushed it to the top of the charts on Audible. I know it was because of his warm endorsement that his audience chose to give my family's story a listen/read. I'm thankful for that.

Since then, I've written a second book and have started my own storytelling podcast. Marty was my first holiday guest when I did a special episode for Thanksgiving in 2023. He gave me a heaping-helping of reasons to be thankful, despite my personal circumstances at the time. I continue to be thankful for Marty's sincere care and concern.

That's why I was honored when he asked if I would be interested in writing a foreword for this new book. It is an honor to do that because, after reading the pre-published copy, I want everyone else to read it, as well. It is a treasure that I expect to be passed from friend to friend with hopeful expectations, thoughtful insights, and possibly new insights.

As we have recently witnessed, the intersection of faith and politics in modern America and Christian circles is seemingly navigated without traffi signals or roundabouts. Without those guardrails and GPS coordinates, it has become a giant traffi jam of unnecessary confusion.

This book is a driver's manual for beginning and experienced drivers of Christianity and worldly considerations. For beginners on their faith journey, it provides expectations and guidelines. For the experienced believer, it offers uncomfortable realities that can only be ignored at great risk to the operator.

As a Christian and keen social observer, Marty can be trusted to provide insights on a variety of contemporary subjects, while remaining faithful to Biblical authority and nuanced rationale. I can probably count on my hands the people I trust enough to say that. That's what this collection of well-written and deeply personal essays provided for me.

I am humbly asking you to give this book a thorough read and examination. I believe strongly that it will bless your life and give you a conversation starter with your family and friends that begins with a good-faith effort to reach reconciliation, not retaliation.

I sincerely hope it blesses you as much as it did me.

Melvin E. Edwards
Author of *The Eyes of Texans: From Slavery to the Texas Capitol* and *The Strength of a Thousand Sons*
Host of the Stories from Real Life podcast

Be in the world, but not of the world. Such a simple thing to hear but not as simple to live. The Christian propensity to slide back into the world from whence we have been saved is a moment-by-moment temptation. God might have saved us out of the miry pit, but like kids on a rainy day we are oft drawn back to the sludge.

Being in the world is not something we can help or change. This earth is our home until the moon or Mars is colonized. But, if they are to be colonized it will be by humans who will merely export this world to those worlds. The moon, with a future population of 200 engineers, scientists, and the rest, will not be a haven of righteousness nor will Mars see the kingdom of God in dusty red. They will be just as much of the world as this one.

Adam and Eve were created for this world. God had his pick of uncountable planets in uncounted galaxies, but formed Earth for the specific purpose of habitation: "For this is what the LORD says—the Creator of the heavens, the God who formed earth and made it, the one who established it (he did not create it to be a wasteland, but formed it to be inhabited)—he says, "I am the LORD and there is no other" (Isaiah 45:18). We can argue for eons whether there is life on *other* planets, but we need to remember *this one* was created to be the home for humanity. This is in every way our home.

The unique adaptiveness of Earth for life is so obvious there is even a science-based philosophical theory which addresses it. It's called the fine-tuning argument.

> *Fine tuning refers to the surprising precision of nature's physical constants and the early conditions of the universe. To explain how a habitable planet like Earth could even exist, these fundamental constants have to be set to just the right values (like tuning a dial to find just the right radio station). If the universe had physical constants with even slightly different values, the universe simply could not support life: it would expand too quickly, or never form carbon atoms, or never make complex molecules like DNA.*[1]

Christian theology agrees. This world was created for life—human, animal, insect—and, to that extent at least, it is our home. We are in the world, or on it if you prefer.

Can we really debate this? If you've ever hiked in the Appalachian Mountain range, felt your ant-like comparison to the Rocky Mountains, seen the incomprehensible expanse of the Pacific Ocean, reveled in the beauty of spring's bloom or autumn's colors you *feel* belonging. Something in us matches what is around us. In so many ways, it feels like home.

But.

Does being in the world, then, mean being of it? Is God talking about physical properties like

Adam created from dust and Eve from Adam? Does being of the world refer to being a carbon-based life form? Our need for water and oxygen to live?

For these reasons and others, many Christians find the concept *of the world* somewhat murky. Most believe the world we are to avoid isn't Earth, like soil and rocks, but something on Earth that affects us, surrounds us, like a fog obscuring our sight but enveloping and chilling us all the while. We have a feeling *the world* is to be avoided, but if it is all around us, how do we avoid it without secluding ourselves from it? What is to be avoided?

Porn? No question that's of the world. Hate? Yeah, that's pretty much a gimme. Playing poker for thousands of dollars? Uh, probably. Playing poker for pennies? Uhm...? Climbing over people on the ladder to success? Yeah, probably so. Fudging the resume to look like a better job applicant? Well... "Little white lies"? Can we just move on now??

In his first epistle, the Apostle John defines the things of the world. He writes, "For all that is in the world—the desire of the fle h, the desire of the eyes, the pride in riches—comes not from the Father, but from the world."[2] But before he defines what's in the world, John starts with this warning: "Do not love the world or the things in the world." Why? What does love for the world indicate, John? "The love of the Father is not in those who love the world."[3] Why? Because the world is "where the devil rules" and is the "sphere of...free operations" of the faithless life.[4]

Oh.

The desire of the flesh can be defined as, "the cravings of sin." That is, temptations and desires that arise from within us because the old self is not fully dead. Though we crucify the old self with its passions and lusts, it routinely climbs off its cross to indulge some sensuous craving. The desire of the eyes "seems to indicate temptations which assault us not only from within, but without through our *eyes*."[5] We can easily recall Eve "seeing" the fruit of the tree and succumbing to temptation. Finally, what the NRSVue translates "the pride in riches" can also refer to all material possessions or the status they bring. The old King James calls it the "pride of life." Rather than the life of the Spirit, the worldly person is ostentatious, pretentious, strutting, showing off, always buying the next newest car, gizmo, house, second house, and on and on, each new purchase merely confirming the lack of satisfaction previous purchases brought.

We should take care not to limit our idea of *the world* to the sins we know from the specific religious group of our upbringing. When I was around thirteen years old, our church called a new pastor. In his theology, if my hair touched my ears or went over my collar, it was a faith matter—a sin. Playing cards—even Gin Rummy and Go Fish—were out, because something something about the Joker card. G-rated movies at the local twin cinema? Not on your life! What if someone thinks you went into the R-rated movie on the other side?? (Never once did we hear, "If you think you see someone doing something wrong, ask them about it. Don't assume the worst.")

Outside the scope of these petty "sins," there was little worldly to be found. Critique of country? Are you kidding? God bless the USA. Exploitation of creation for greed and profi ? It's all gonna burn anyway, so who cares? Questions about (or God forbid *protesting*) America's wars? You unpatriotic-commie-hippie-pinko...longhair.

One steadfast problem in the American expression of the church is our segmentation of *the world* into what is acceptable and what is not. Our preferred sins, the ones we don't think affect us in any negative way are okay. The ones we find really dirty—those sins *they* do—are the ones to be avoided. (*They* being anyone not *us*.)

But everywhere we look we see what it means to be *of the world*. Attitudes and actions that don't reflect the kingdom of God, i.e., that are not a fruit of his Spirit. These "works of the fle h," as the Apostle Paul calls them elsewhere, are what God tells us to avoid.[6]

What if we gave ourselves a stare in the mirror? We might find we have shifted the goalposts. We've rewritten God's commands as a law we can live with comfortably; one that doesn't tweak our consciences or prick our hearts. We're of the world—but with plausible deniability.

The essays that follow attempt to explore a few of the complexities that come from trying to be in the world but not of the world. It isn't comprehensive; I'm not trying to cover all the bases in the entire major leagues. I only want to think better, more biblically, about *the world* and what it means to be in it, not of it. If it helps you think better, too, I'll be all the more content.

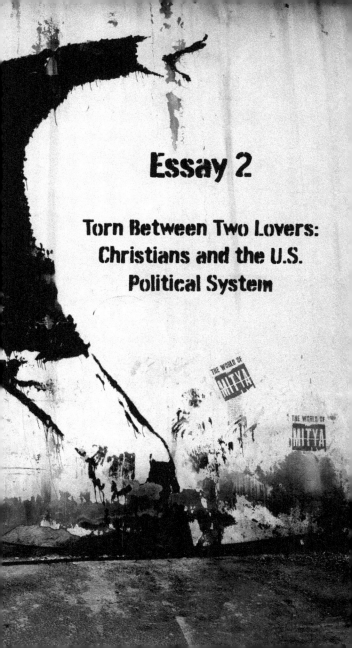
Essay 2

Torn Between Two Lovers: Christians and the U.S. Political System

It's common now to hear people say, "I'm politically homeless." I've heard it so often now it's practically a truism if not cliché. Many Christians feel the two-party political scheme of Democrats and Republicans has become enough of a non-choice at voting time that writing-in the neighbor's dog would be as effect ve as anyone on the ballot.

Especially at the top.

For the last several elections, after the Democratic and Republican conventions, folks ask, "Is this the best we can do?" Or, "Out of all Americans, we can't fi ld two better candidates?" We suffer through so many rounds of "lesser of two evils" we can hardly distinguish the good from the evil. Even worse is the danger of becoming so enamored with the lesser evil it eventually appears to us as righteous.

As of this writing, the renowned Country music artist Kris Kristofferson has recently died. In response to a question in a 1990s interview with fellow "Highwaymen" Willie Nelson, Johnny Cash, and Waylon Jennings, Kristofferson complained America actually has a one-party system. In so saying, he echoed the great African-American thinker and author, W.E.B. DuBois, who wrote in 1956, "I believe that democracy has so far disappeared in the United States that no 'two evils' exist. There is but one evil party with two names." Thus, the feeling of political homelessness acknowledged back then is still felt by many in 2024.

But, just perhaps, being politically homeless is not a bad thing. Perhaps, if Christians judge our moment in time correctly, we will better understand we have no political home, nor need to seek one, precisely because this is not our home. This is not an argument to abstain from politics, but to raise the possibility that to understand politics rightly and practice it righteously requires us to prioritize it properly. If we feel at home in politics or make our bed in the houses of Democrats, Republicans, Libertarians, or Greens, we are liable to wake up with fleas if not an STD—Spiritually Transmitted Disease.

When faced with the opportunity to trade his own kingdom for "all the kingdoms of the world," Jesus chose his; a kingdom of love, service, humility, and righteousness. When challenged by the Roman procurator, Pontius Pilate, Jesus affirme that his kingdom is not of this world. If it were of this world, his disciples would have taken up arms against the Romans. When one of his disciples, Peter, did in fact take up a sword against a Roman soldier, Jesus rebuked Peter and healed the soldier. A starker contrast of Jesus' kingdom ethics and purpose could hardly be requested.

Since Jesus never instructed his followers to build a home in politics, we should be wary of picking up our tools to that end. Yet, being involved in politics is not the same as being subservient to it. Whatever Christians might seek to gain in the political sphere or whatever influence we might seek to hold, we must remember the political constructs are of this world by definition. The Church is the Kingdom preview, Congress is not. At its very best, politics is a tool God can use to bear witness to his righteousness and justice. At its worst, politics is God's competitor, substituting human wisdom and self-righteousness for God's own. And, as experience has shown us, American politics is usually a slide to the very deepest valley.

The writer of Hebrews tells us Abraham lived in a tent in the Promised Land while looking forward to a city God had built. Later in the same chapter, heroes of faith are lauded because they "confessed" their sojourn on Earth was only temporary. They were "seeking a homeland" and it was not where they came from; nor was it where they were tenting. It was "a better place—a heavenly one" (Hebrews 11:8–10, 13–16). Here, there, earth, heaven; the moment-to-moment pull tests our loyalty. "To be a stranger, alien, sojourner, or pilgrim means that our sense of belonging to God will exist with some level of tension with our immediate home."[7] So, we oft need reminding this world is not our permanent home.

But, the U.S. political system is not God's way of reminding.

When God's people understand God's kingdom, politics is a means to this end: displaying the righteousness of God and pursuing biblical justice in society for the good of our neighbor. "Good practices lead us in the direction of seeking justice and defending the oppressed, goals with unavoidably political dimensions."[8] When God's people conflate God's kingdom with worldly dominions, trade spiritual power attained by faith for temporal power attained by back-biting and back-stabbing, the result is a form of godliness with divine power denied. Not only are the works of the Spirit traded for the works of the fle h, the works of the fle h are deemed spiritual and the spiritual works useless. Temporal power—at whatever cost—becomes both the means and the end; the glory of God rejected for a wobbly seat at a worldly table. The Christian politician, rather than being a seeker of power, should be a "bearer of principles."[9]

Still, easier said than done.

In the year of our Lord, two thousand twenty-four, the United States plays host to a political system dominated by the Republican Party and the Democratic Party. Can anyone alive today remember a time when more than two parties were competitive all up and down ballots from city council to the White House? It is certain no one alive today can remember a Whig or Democratic-Republican president in Washington.[10] As such, the temptation to grab onto one of our two major parties or their candidates and hold on for dear life provides too ready a choice. Political parties stoke feelings of social insecurity, fear of "the other," and dread of the future. They idolize personal autonomy, normalize lust for political power, and champion unbiblical national interests. Parties, intentional or not, invoke a sense of community; a place to belong. Why else are hats, shirts, mugs, watches, shoes, bumper stickers, and Bibles hawked by vendors and campaign websites? These are attempts to exploit group dynamics for votes. But should Christians *belong* to these communities? Do Christians belong to *anything* worldly?

Christians can rightfully wonder (perhaps should rightfully wonder) whether we should adopt terminology like, "I'm a Republican," "I'm a Democrat," "I'm a Libertarian," or "I'm a Green." What worldy identifier is worth trading a biblical identifier like *disciple of Jesus*? What shall it profit a man or woman if they should gain the whole party but lose their soul? Jesus' disciple Matthew was a tax collector, a collaborator with the Roman occupation government. His disciple Simon was a Zealot, a Jewish citizen dedicated to overthrowing Rome's domination. We know this because they are so identified in the lists of the Twelve recorded in the early ministry of Jesus. Yet, aside from these introductions, their politics are never emphasized; only the Kingdom is. The rest of the New Testament places no emphasis on political pursuit or goals. No one is encouraged to seek a Senate seat, but to pray for those who have them.

On the other hand, Abraham Kuyper, a Dutch Christian, pastor, and theologian, founded a political party he hoped would maintain the biblical value of justice. The Anti-Revolutionary Party, founded in 1879, was the world's first Christian democratic party. The word Christian denoted not an evangelistic, conversionist goal of bringing unbelieving citizens to faith through politics. Rather, "it aspired to implement a vision of justice for all fl wing out of that faith."[11] Kuyper's vision wasn't a Christian takeover of government, but Christian influence promoting fairness to all from within government.

The difficultie in replicating Kuyper in America today are manifold. Voters are not Democrat or Republican by tradition; few are voting for the party of their grandparents. Voters, even Christian voters, cling to multiple planks of each major party. If you value little to no immigration, "small government," lots of defense spending, and certain conservative social values, you'll likely vote Republican. If you value bodily autonomy (especially female), government action in helping the poor, comprehensive immigration reform, and gun control laws, you'll likely vote Democrat. These are issues largely sustained by the two parties and over which millions of Christians often seem to prefer disagreement, even antagonism, toward brothers and sisters in Christ. Witness the struggle of the American Solidarity Party to gain any traction. ASP is a recently created party, ostensibly holding Christian values—or at least Christian-derived values. The party platform crosses lines between Democrat and Republican priorities. While I will admit that only a few years cannot tell the story of the party's future, ASP has yet to attract enough Christian interest to have candidates in every state or their 2024 presidential ticket on each state's ballot. At least part of the challenge for ASP is party-tied Christians believing their current party is Christian enough *and has realistic chances to win*, not merely bring future change. When every election is "the most important election of our lifetime" there's little time or interest in considering 20 or 30 years down the road.

Republicans believe another Democratic administration will bring the end of the world as we know it. Democrats believe another Trump administration will bring the end of the world as we know it. And God's saying, "Y'all...I feel fine"

Christians will do well recapturing the biblical truth that God's priority is *his* kingdom. Jesus' first sermon concerned the good news of the kingdom of God. Christ went, accompanied by the Twelve, among cities and towns preaching the good news of the kingdom of God (Luke 8:1). Jesus said preaching the good news of the kingdom of God was the purpose of his coming (Luke 4:43). Salvation came in the book of Acts as Phillip preached the good news of the kingdom of God (Acts 8:12). Jesus' entire earthly ministry embodied and messaged his kingdom; there was no other theme. Though the kingdom would grow like yeast, the Savior never taught his disciples— neither the Twelve nor the multitude—to set up a shadow government. Though the kingdom has a King, that King would not be installed by force to a temporal throne. His kingdom—unlike political parties, all of which eventually be ashes and dust—has no end.

What would happen if Christians in America spurned their political lovers and returned, as Jesus once implored a church, to our first love? I mean, truly, not just talking the talk. What would happen if churches in America became known by our love for one another and for those who do not know Christ rather than love for power and position? What might happen if we lived according to our Kingdom citizenship rather than political partisanship? What would happen if we kept our relationship to politics in its proper place, the kingdoms of this world in their proper place, and rejected the ways of the world that, lacking an eternal perspective, prioritize both? It might be that we never repent; we never prioritize the Kingdom; we never know what could happen.

But it is time we find out

Essay 3

Let's Love First

The Year of Our Lord 2016

After the horrific attack on the Pulse Nightclub, Orlando in which 49 people were murdered and another 50+ injured a lot of people are talking about mourning with those who mourn, and rightly so. This is biblical counsel.

Others direct our focus to loving and caring for the families left behind, and those from the community of the fallen. In Orlando, it was the gay community. In Charleston the Christian community. In Oregon the educational community. In Newtown the local community. And on and on.

Many have offered help to the community of Orlando. Chick-Fil-A opened on Sunday to provide meals to families, workers, and blood donors. Other restaurants did the same.

Grace Church of Orlando and First Baptist Orlando are hosting a community prayer service tonight, and other churches and organizations are mobilizing to help families and friends.

Followers of Jesus are eager to demonstrate love in the aftermath of this horrific act

But, some are not impressed. Perhaps it's the rawness of the moment. Perhaps it's just suppressed feelings boiling over. Perhaps it's that we haven't listened as intently as we should. The truth remains: many people aren't impressed with love after the fact.

Love after the fact is too easily attributed to a guilty conscience. Love after the fact is too easily seen as an attempt to wipe ourselves clean. Love after the fact is too easily seen as insincere.

What then? Why not love firs ?

Why not love first since He first loved us? (1 John 4:19)

Why not love first since love is the fulfillment of the law? (Romans 13:10)

Why not love first since we are commanded to love our neighbor as ourselves? (Mark 12:31)

Why not love first because this is love: not that we loved God, but that He loved us and gave His Son to be an offering for our sin ? (1 John 4:10)

Why not love first since it is the reason God gave His one and only Son for the sins of the world? (John 3:16)

Why not love first since the love of God has been poured out in our hearts? (Romans 5:5)

Why not love first since God demonstrated His love in the giving of Jesus? (Romans 5:8)

Why not love first since we're supposed to love even our enemies, and most of the people we are called to love are not that? (Luke 6:27)

Why not love first because God is love? (1 John 4:8)

It is not that our love re-does what Jesus did; those things are already done. It truly is fini hed. But when we love as God loves we embody the love that accomplished those things.

Yes, there will be some who think love means we approve of all the content in life's closets. Yes, there will be those who insist it is hypocrisy to say "I love you" without condemning behavior they believe to be wrong. But, we make zero progress if we spend all our time arguing that we do love when we have the option of showing it fervently and continuously. Love, not debate, is the great convincer.

Loving those who are least like me is when I am most like Christ.

I would guess, on the whole, we tend to be more expert in loving the *things* of the world, which is forbidden, than we are at loving the *people* of the world, which is commanded.

Some time ago, after writing an article entitled "For God so Loved Caitlyn Jenner,"[12] I wrote a follow-up to address some expressed concerns as to how Christians should love. Part of it read:

> *Jesus regularly appeared condemnable to reach people who were condemned. It is easy for us to look back 2,000 years later and say, "Oh, that's why Jesus did that." His immediate audience, though, did not always understand what He was doing. Sometimes it looked like Jesus was sinning while Jesus was saving. Even the Twelve periodically stopped to ask, "Hey, uh, what exactly was that all about?"*
>
> *Talking to the woman at the well, touching the unclean, being touched by the unclean, being crucified—all of these acts gave a questionable public appearance.*

We love to talk about the woman at the well, don't we? Jesus confronts the woman about her sinfulness. She nearly always makes an appearance in modern discussions.

What we often overlook is the length to which Jesus had put His reputation at risk before He ever "confronted her" about her sin. He interacted with a woman who was a Samaritan, a woman, and a woman with a sordid sexual past and present. All three of these were taboos for Jewish rabbis. When the disciples returned from seeking food, even they were shocked that Jesus talked to her at all.

In fact, if we look at the ministry of Jesus, He seemed to have tenderness for people who had sexual struggles. He was approachable. He did not gain this reputation by using, "You're a perv" for an opening line. The woman at the well, the woman caught in adultery, the woman who anointed His feet were all people who had sexual issues.

We err if we think Jesus was only demeaned in becoming sin for us. Jesus not only bore our sins in His death; He often bore our disrepute in His life.[13]

Here is a shocker: we can learn a lot from Jesus, not just *whether* to love, but *how* to love. This is a place where we disciples need to be more like the Master.

Let's love first

A lot has happened in eight years. It's now 2024 and the idea of "loving firs " seems a nostalgic relic of a past long abandoned, like Father Knows Best or Family Matters. America is divided right down its red and blue gut. Trust barely exists, neither from the populace to the governing body, nor from the Right to the Left, nor from "us" to those who are not like "us," nor the political pollsters that ostensibly help us anticipate political race outcomes. God help if it takes another terrorist attack to bring people together for survival, much less to love one another.

Perhaps the most popular section of scripture read at Christian weddings is from 1 Corinthians 13, an exposition of how love expresses itself to others. It surely applies to marriage, but nowhere in the text does marriage get even an honorable mention. Paul insists that love is superior, in all ways, to what the Corinthian believers esteemed most highly. He writes,

Love is patient, love is kind. Love does not envy, is not boastful, is not arrogant, is not rude, is not self-seeking, is not irritable, and does not keep a record of wrongs. Love finds no joy in unrighteousness but rejoices in the truth. It bears all things, believes all things, hopes all things, endures all things. Love never ends. (vs 4–8)

It takes no imagination to grasp the fact that compared to 1 Corinthians, we usually fail to love first. We fail to love those with whom we disagree politically opting for argument and judgment instead. We fail to love those who differ from us racially, economically, socially, and spiritually, choosing our tribal comfort instead. We fail to love the least of these in our cities and towns whether unborn, just born, or growing in wisdom and stature, leaning instead into politicians and parties who will bring about less change than we could if we but tried.

Love is patient with the hurting, the addicted, and the traumatized.

Love is kind to immigrants.

Love is not envious of the rich.

Love does not boast of privilege.

Love does not lord arrogantly over the dispossessed.

Love is not rude to those who struggle with a specific langua e.

Love does not say "my way or the highway."

Love is not irritated by those who don't get it.

Love does not keep a scorecard of being sinned against.

Love is not happy when evil happens to anyone, even evildoers.

Love loves the truth.

Loves holds up under all weight.

Love keeps the faith.

Love keeps hoping.

Love endures the deepest valleys and longest nights.

Love does not end.

Love isn't easy, but it's the way of Jesus. If his people desire to be like him, we have no option but to love.

So, let's love first

I have two tattoos. That's probably where it will end.

On my left forearm are the words, "Would it help?" I took the phrase from Steven Spielberg's excellent movie, Bridge of Spies, a "based on a true story" tale of trading spy and student for spy during the Cold War. Tom Hanks plays attorney James Donovan who is assigned representation of suspected Soviet spy Rudolf Abel (Mark Rylance) in a slightly-less-than-above-board-attempt to show our justice system superior to the communists'. Since a guilty verdict is assured, each bit of news relayed from attorney to client is bad. When Abel responds each time with "okay," Donovan, nonplussed, asks, "Aren't you worried?" Abel replies simply, "Would it help?"

Would it help? is for me a modern take on the Beatitudes: "Do not worry. Not about height, hair, food, clothes, or anything else. *None of you by worrying can change these things.*"

On my right forearm are the Latin words, *Momento Tempus. Momento Aeternum*. Literally, remember temporality remember eternity. Using dynamic equivalence it's: *Remember you are temporal. Remember you are eternal*. It is a constant reminder that I live in two worlds—a fleeting world and an eternal world. I am of time and not-time. I exist in a realm where death is the inevitable outcome and in a realm where life is the only outcome. I am of the visible and the invisible, the bound and the unbound, the time-constrained and the clock-less,

I am temporal and I am eternal. *Momento Tempus. Momento Aeternum.*

The challenge, of course, in this tension is the temporal is seen and the eternal is not. It is easy, even natural, to focus on what is at hand. Literally. I can pick up a book; I can't see an angel. I can drive my truck; I can't see a chariot of fire. I can *do* mercy; I can't *see* it. The contrast fills one's life. The Bible mentions it specifi ally in 2 Corinthians 4:18, "So we do not focus on what is seen, but on what is unseen. For what is seen is temporary, but what is unseen is eternal." In the 1st century, millennia before the advent of the Distracted Age, God's people were reminded not to count on the things they could count. Don't focus on your sheep, goats, cows, homestead, or garments; those might be needed for life but they are not life. Focus on heavenly things where Christ sits at the right hand of God (Colossians 3:1). If first century Christians with their minimal earthly possessions, needed reminding of temporality's dangers, how much more we of hand-held computers, clothes-stuffed closets, in-ground pools, multiple autos, and big, bigger, biggest-screen TVs? Temporal gravitation pull has increased from Newton's apple to Bolton's black hole.[14]

Yet, the life of faith does not ignore the temporal; time is where faith is exhibited. The life of faith recognizes this temporary, physical world was created by *he who is* and from *that which is* invisible (Hebrews 11:3). In the pantheon of faithful biblical characters, Abel feared God (eternal) so offered an acceptable sacrifice (temporal). Noah, warned by God (eternal), built an ark (temporal). Abraham sought a heavenly homeland (eternal) while sojourning to an earthly one (temporal). James K. A. Smith, on Ecclesiastes 3:13, says, "The teacher's counsel is provocative, even table-turning: lean into your creaturehood; live into your temporality; dig into your toil."[15] Biblical Christians are not "so heavenly minded they are no earthly good" as the old preacher-saying goes. Remembering eternity does not negate temporality; it tempers it.

In *Mind and Cosmos*, philosopher Thomas Nagel writes,

> *We and other creatures with mental lives are organisms, and our mental capacities apparently depend on our physical constitution. So what explains the existence of organisms like us must also explain the existence of mind. But if the mental is not itself merely physical, it cannot be fully explained by physical science. And then, as I shall argue, it is difficult to avoid the conclusion that those aspects of our physical constitution that bring with them the mental cannot be fully explained by physical science either.*[16]

Nagel concludes, not from religious belief but from biological evidence, that the human mind and consciousness cannot be explained by physical science alone because they aren't merely physical. And if not merely physical then then not merely temporal. The philosopher knocks on eternity's door.

Momento Aeternum raises the question, "How does what I'm doing impact eternity, either for myself or others?" If an unbelieving friend or neighbor sees me do X, is their mind turned toward or away from an awaiting eternity? If a believing friend or family member hears a certain tone of voice, do they see evidence of eternity in my heart or just another discordant, loveless gong among so many? Followers of Jesus are the people in time who bear witness to eternity; science does not. Religions focused on meditation and escaping the world do not. Those who depend on the unpredictable whims of unpredictable deities do not. Those who have been instructed, "Set your minds on things above" (Colossians 3:2), "Do not worry about tomorrow (Matthew 6:34), and that our lives "do not consist in the amount of things we possess" (Luke 12:15), should be those whose very lives point not only to a better way but to a better place.

Yet, not a better *time*.

It is difficul for mere mortals afflicte with temporality as we are to imagine eternity. An old gospel song says, speaking of heaven, "What a wonderful time we'll have up there." The colloquialism refers to a joyous event that occupies a chunk of time. Similarly, "We all had a great time." But we will not have a wonderful *time* in eternity. *Time* is a failed referent. No amount of time describes or even opens a window on eternity. What might? A millennium? We've had plenty of those. A century? Not even a speed bump. As I was working on this essay, my wife told me one of the last remaining World War 2 Navajo Code Talkers died at 107 years of age. Is that a long *time*? Only for those bound in it. No amount of time is a long time compared to eternity, the place without time.

Christians understand heaven as being in the presence of God. Most have read or heard there is no night there because Jesus himself is the light (Revelation 21:23). The function of the sun and moon to provide light is rendered superfluous by the Lamb's radiant glory. But we still have trouble transcribing this into timelessness. Is it like Al Pacino in Christopher Nolan's brilliant *Insomnia*, with its troubled detective unable to fall asleep in the Land of the Midnight Sun? Is heaven occupied by millions of sleep-deprived saints? No one thinks that. But what do we think?

Perhaps the difficult lies in we can't fully jettison concepts of time for not-time. We hardly have adequate language to refer to eternity without reference to time: "It's when time is no more." or "It's when time never ends." Even the use of *when* betrays us. We're merely placing eternity along a timeline however long it might be. Maybe, instead, it will help to think of eternity as a place.

If Nagel is right, and the physical cannot fully explain the mind, then, to steal from C. S. Lewis, perhaps we were made for another world, one that is not physical; or at least the physical is not its defining element. After Jesus rose from the dead in what theologians call his "glorified" body, he was still able to eat fi h. He was still able to take bread and wine. Yet he was also able to appear in a room without using the door, vanish from a room in an instant, and ascend into the heavens on a cloud. What is physical about him after the resurrection is also eternal, apparently not held in the space/time continuum. Rather than the temporal being the natural, the reality most easily lived, the eternal is now the dominant feature of the body and of life. Thus, "eternal life" refers to a quality of life, not simply a quantity of it.

Which brings us back to remembering we are both temporal and eternal, of this earth and of heaven. When we live by faith in the eternal world, eternity breaks through into time. Like the saints of old, "by faith" we bring the eternal into the temporal. We are temporal; our opportunities on earth to demonstrate the life of Christ are limited by time. Yet, we are eternal; our existence does not stop here, our experience is not limited by this life, and our end is not a calendar date. We are both.

Momento Tempus. Momento Aeternum. Amen.

Essay 5

A Few Thoughts about Food and Eating

The Year of our Lord 2023

"Food is God's love made nutritious and delicious."

~Norman Wirzba, theologian[17]

"Most people don't give much thought to food as long as it's there and it doesn't cost too much."

~Shane Burchfi l, Tennessee farmer[18]

What if food matters and not simply to fill our bellies. What if food reveals something of God to us. What if, instead of shoveling anything and near everything into our mouths, too hurriedly to ask what it is and too distracted to care what it was, we understood food and eating as parts and acts of worship, or at the least, acknowledgment of good things that come from the Father of Lights (James 3).

The concept of a book came one day as I was "saying grace" over lunch. I began to think about the words a suburbanite like myself recites when praying over a meal.

"Thank you for this food you have provided." "Thank you for your many blessings." "Bless this food and the hands that prepared it."

Then I thought about how the same words would have meant something different years ago to a farmer raising his family on food they themselves had raised. His wife and children who joined him in the fi ld planting after the vernal equinox, then harvesting beans, peas, tomatoes, and grains from late summer into fall. Grateful at mealtime for blessings they had planted, tended, picked, hulled, washed, and prepared; cows they had pastured; hogs they had slopped; goats they had milked; and hen's eggs gathered morning-by-morning.

In between planting in the hopeful spring and the long harvest sun, farmer's eyes turned skyward, emotions ranging between anticipation and anxiety about rains that came too early, too late, just as needed, or not at all. Concerns about pests for which poisons did not yet exist, at the mercy of scavenging hordes of vegetarians on the wing who could decimate a crop, consuming in minutes what had taken months for the gestating ground to birth. Animals, some named, loved, and nurtured from infancy, led daily from barn to yard or pasture and returned at evening to same, fed as needed, protected when threatened, then, eventually, sacrificed into chops, hams, roasts, steaks, ribs, bacon, sausage, drumsticks, and breasts, wings, and neck-bones, providing what the family needed and, perhaps, selling the rest.

"Thank you for this food you have provided," means something different coming from my tongue when the sum total of my anxiety is waiting too long to find a parking space at Kroger, where I soon roam—in cool, blissful air-conditioning—for shiny fruits and vegetables, selected, packaged, wrapped, waxed, arranged—utterly detached from the earth from whence they sprang, the farmers that grew them, the machines—or humans—that harvested them, the warehouses that stored them, and the trucks that delivered them, and retaining only a paycheck relationship to the Produce Department employees who stocked them. A child could be forgiven for not knowing apples, oranges, celery, and ginger root do not grow on shelves or that eggs don't arrive on earth in cartons, free of feathers, hay, and excrement.

"This food you have provided," indeed.

> *The more divorced we are from the cultivation of crops and animals, and the more mechanical and manufactured our food appears to us, the less we see it as a gift. When our meals come to us carefully wrapped in paper from hands wrapped in latex gloves that took ingredients from hermetically sealed plastic bags that were created in a sanitary, automated factory, it is no easy thing to see the hand of God at work providing for us. Contingencies of weather and seasons, human error, and animal behavior and health have been carefully, systematically, and technologically reduced as much as possible... Humanity has mastered nature, and we owe humanity no gratitude—just some monetary compensation.*[19]

It is not the fault of the average eater that the industrial revolution, having produced mechanization and perfected production turned its focus from inanimate objects like steel and plastic to those with life and breath like chickens and pigs. The results have not been stellar. We are certainly no closer to Eden; we might actually be closer to Sodom.

Farmer/philosopher Joel Salatin notes:

> *What happens when you don't ask: how do we make pigs happy? Well, you view the pig as just a pile of protoplasmic structure to be manipulated however cleverly human hubris can imagine to manipulate it. And when you view life from that kind of mechanistic, arrogant, disrespectful standpoint, you very soon begin to view all of life from a very disrespectful, arrogant, manipulative standpoint. And the fact is, we aren't machines.*[20]

I'm just supposing here, but maybe trying to build food like Mercedes builds a turbodiesel is not what God had in mind when he commanded "Let the earth produce vegetation: seed-bearing plants and fruit trees" and "let the animals produce after their own kind" (Genesis 1:11).

What if eating is more than masticating a leaf of lettuce or kernel of corn until it is sufficientl reduced from its original form to swallow and digest it. If meals are to be more than nutrient pit-stops, what else "more" might they be? What if we didn't speed through mealtime like a culinary Indy 500, the checkered flag a clean plate and hopefully a clean shirt, too.

What if we expected of mealtime what God expects of mealtime, which, as we discover in the Bible's pages, is what Jesus experienced at mealtime. Jesus showed us what God would do all the time, including when food was involved: enough food, not enough food, more of the same kind of food, unexpected food, unexpected drink. Jesus' cousin, John the Baptizer, lived a life of culinary austerity ("he came neither eating nor drinking"), but Jesus came both eating and drinking. The Baptizer was said to have a demon; the Son was said to be a glutton.

If you can't beat'em, you might as well eat.

Jesus showed us not only how to relate to food, he showed us who we could eat it with. Jesus ate with the religious and the irreligious, the unrighteous and the self-righteous (who were also unrighteous, it just wasn't as obvious), the Pharisees and prostitutes, the proud and the penitent. He was nothing if not an indiscriminate feaster. If holy living means avoiding the riff-ra , sexually problematic, thieves, political turncoats, frauds, and other sinners, Jesus didn't make the grade. And to most of the religious leaders, he didn't. In the eyes of the religiarchy, being a friend of sinners disqualified you from being a friend of God. Jesus turned that on its head and regularly used meals to do so. To him, it seems, one cannot be a friend of God unless he or she is a friend of sinners as well. Indeed, in the gospels we find sinner, saint, and Sovereign together at the table.

Mealtime does not appear to have been an outlier for Jesus. He did not squeeze in a rushed All-You-Can-Eat at the Galilee Catfi h House before the next round of sermons, healings, deliverances, and raisings-from-the-dead. Mealtime was a feature of his earthly ministry. He fully embraced eating, drinking, reclining, and conversation. He used meals as teaching times. He referred to himself as water, wine, and bread. Jesus was no gnostic; he embraced the physical nature of food and drink and seems to have overjoyed himself in doing so.

Jesus' earliest disciples integrated food into their Christian experience. Daily, records Luke, they were breaking bread from house to house. While they filled their stomachs, they prayed and studied the apostles' teaching. Arguably, food brought them together with teaching as a bonus, rather than teaching bringing them together with sandwiches along for the ride. What if we have it backward? Should meals be as much the glue that holds fellowship together as the preaching and praying? (In a moment of candor, pastors might admit the Fifth Sunday Dinner has at least as much allure as the other four Sundays' sermons.)

The Lord's Supper in the early church was not a ten-minute addendum to the end of a Sunday service or a serve-yourself "Communion Snackable" of stale bread and decommissioned wine for attendees inclined to partake. The

Lord's Supper was the focal point of the Christian gathering with "the Lord" as host; it was his supper. If we observe it properly, it still is. But most don't. Alan Streett writes in *Subversive Meals*, "A modern-day communion service in which a symbolic piece of cracker and a thimble-sized portion of wine are distributed to the faithful had no counterpart in the firs -century church".[21] Perhaps our loss of connection to food and meals is related to our incomplete practice of the Lord's Supper, producing a void in our Christian experience both deep and wide.

Having lost the Kingdom perspective of Eden's plenty, it is little surprise we have lost the connection of the earth to farming, of farming to food production, of food production to meals, and of meals to Heaven. At each course along the way, we see the temporal substituted for the eternal, exploitation rather than blessing. In his quaint memoir, *The Land Remembers: A Story of a Farm and Its People*, Ben Logan writes about his father's decision to stop growing tobacco on their hilltop Wisconsin farm:

> *Tobacco had been alien to us. I don't think it had anything to do with whether or not is was right to smoke—Father liked a good cigar. But it may have had something to do with a larger, more subtle morality. Other crops completed the cycle from growth to new growth with enough of the crop going back to the land in manure or waste to see the*

> *soil healthy. Other crops worked with the land, building it. Tobacco used up the land.*[22]

Like Logan's perception of tobacco, the Fall in every way uses up food and mealtime leaving depletion rather than meaning behind. There is indeed a morality in play—perhaps not so subtle.

Preparation, appreciation, taste, fellowship, conversation, laughter, and aromas remind us of the blessings of God and the fellowship he offers. The way many of us in the West eat and experience meals no longer reflects this. We often treat meals as a necessary, but unwanted intrusion into our otherwise productive lives. Fast food culture diminishes the importance of slowing down to savor what is before us; urban and suburban living and "invented, packaged food" obscures for many Christians the mystery of planting, praying, growing, and harvesting. Technology distracts us when we are together for meals, fragmenting what should be a holy experience. In some parts of the world, agriculture is suffering due to unfavorable growing conditions (attributed in some cases to a changing climate) leaving residents with an uncertain future. Poverty makes it near impossible for many to afford good food, forcing choices between varying degrees of nutritional paucity.

Have too many Christians lost the connection between meals and the Kingdom of God, ignoring whether our physical bodies have become in some ways detached from our spiritual lives, forming a sort of accidental Gnosticism? We don't deny the reality of the physical, but we distance it from the spiritual in ways that harm both. This is true especially where food, eating, and meals are involved. May those among God's people who never have to wonder where their next meal will come from, strive to recover a biblically-informed appreciation for food and meals, so we may better celebrate through them the good God who provides both so that our next supper is different than our last one

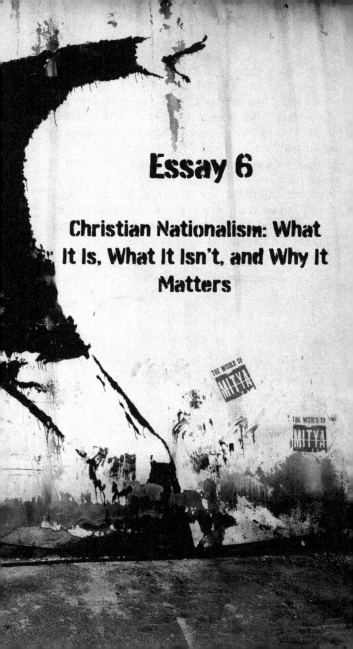

Essay 6

Christian Nationalism: What It Is, What It Isn't, and Why It Matters

The Year of Our Lord 2022

When I started this article on Christian Nationalism, I did not have in mind that January 6, the first anniversary of the Election Fraud Hoax Insurrection, was just around the corner.

A recent topic *de jour* of the evangelical Internet is Christian Nationalism. From those who decry it as an unholy hybrid of faith and state to those who defend it as, more or less, Christian citizenship, Christian Nationalism is the latest shell fired in the culture wars. My first attempt to address Christian Nationalism went like this:

> *This unhealthy, unholy hybrid of Christianity and hyper-nationalism has cheapened the former and lent unwarranted authority to the latter. When a church baptizes converts under the American flag—as I personally witnessed one July 4—it is Christians, not unbelievers, who have more than their toes in the waters of blasphemy.*

As tends to happen in these battles, definitions are few, assumptions are prevalent, tribal alliances are fast, and clarity-seeking passé, leaving too many ended where they started, only more certain of their position.

What follows is offered toward clarity, with defined terms, to the end that Christianity is detached from nationalism as the kingdom of our God and of his Christ is separate and distinct from any kingdom of man no matter how splendiferous, religious, or long-lived.

First, what Christian Nationalism is not. It is not another name for patriotism. Patriotism, per Merriam-Webster, is love for or devotion to one's country. Country in this context is more than geographic boundaries. Patriotic Canadians need not love a shared border with the United States; indeed, some might prefer not to. "Country" includes the culture(s), language(s), history, geography, and symbols of a people in a land-space controlled by its own government.

People along political and ideological spectrums can love their country. Some love their country because of what it has been; others because of what it can become. But many (if not most) love what they *perceive their country to be* rather than what it is. One difference between nationalism and patriotism is the latter does not require an *other*; it can exist without reference to being first, better than, or extra. A patriot can live in a country of no power just as well as a superpower, as every Olympiad reminds us.

Similarly, some insist Christian Nationalism is nothing more than love of neighbor, but this is woefully insufficient It was the Pharisees who tried to trip Jesus by asking, "Who is my neighbor?" Jesus' distilled answer is, "Whoever needs help or helps."

Others argue, "Shouldn't we love the people that are near us more than people who are far away," as if I can't love a good friend in California or Romania more than someone on the other side of my neighborhood that I have never met. Proximity might lead to more frequent interaction, but it might not; it definit ly does not lead to more love. Plenty of Christians who love their country don't know anything about the people on their street.

Some contend that Christian Nationalism is the same as being a Christian citizen, that to oppose Christian Nationalism is to be gnostic or to otherwise ignore the physical world. Such a contention reveals an inaccurate understanding of nationalism and Christian Nationalism, both of which are hyper-focused on their own country to the near or total exclusion of other countries. For Christian Nationalists the other countries of the world may as well be ether if they conflict with the purposes and goals of the Nationalist's homeland.

Before we address what Christian Nationalism is, let's look at a distinction between nationalism and Christian Nationalism. One can be a nationalist and not be a Christian. Both the Nazi Party and the Soviets were nationalists. Torch-carrying Alt-Right protestors chanting "Blood and Soil" are nationalists. The Tamil Tigers were nationalists. Nationalism does not entail violence (though violence often accompanies it), nor does it need a specific religious impulse. It can be distinctly secular.

Ernest Gellner, the late Director of the Centre for the Study of Nationalism at Central European University and author of *Nations and Nationalism*, defines nationalism as "primarily a principle that holds that the political and national unit should be congruent," though he accepts a slightly expanded definition as "the striving to make culture and polity congruent, to endow a culture with its own political roof, and not more than one roof at that."[23]

Emeritus Professor of Nationalism and Ethnicity at the London School of Economics, Anthony D. Smith, says nationalism is an "ideological movement for attaining and maintaining autonomy, unity and identity for a population which some of its members deem to constitute an actual or potential nation."[24]

Adam Wyatt, author of *Biblical Patriotism: An Evangelical Alternative to Nationalism*, writes, "Nationalism is the thesis that a person's first and supreme loyalty should be to the nation-state."[25] And, "Nationalism is connected to a people's relationship with their community and country, and it is an irreplaceable and vital part of their identity."[26] It is *America First* and any other slogan like it.

Finally, conservative theologian and writer, Bruce Ashford, writes in his article "The (Religious) Problem with Nationalism":

> *In the modern West, political nationalism centers on modern nation-states. Nationalists view their nation-*

> *state as more than merely the aggregate of its citizens. Usually, the nation is seen as superior to other nation-states in its ability to exemplify some transcendent value. For Americans, this value is usually freedom.*[27]

(Aside: Ashford addresses a crucial point. America's highest value is freedom, a value that Christianity teaches is subordinate to loving and serving others. Followers of Jesus have been freed *to do* those things, not freed *to avoid* them.)

Christian Nationalism is a form of Nationalism that has been baptized and sanctified by Christian theology. It is the position that one's country is superior to all other countries due to a perceived unique relationship to God and/or a conflation of Christian doctrine with the laws/policies of the country. Joseph Williams of Rutgers University defines Christian ationalists as those who

> *insist that the United States was established as an explicitly Christian nation, and they believe that this close relationship between Christianity and the state needs to be protected—and in many respects restored—in order for the U.S. to fulfill its God-given destiny.*[28]

In *Kierkegaard's Critique of Christian Nationalism*, Stephen Backhouse defines CN as "the family or set of ideas or assumption by which one's belief in the development and uniqueness of one's national group (usually accompanied by claims of superiority) is combined with, or underwritten by, Christian theology and practice."[29]

Of late, academics Andrew Whitehead and Sam Perry have helped shift the Christian Nationalism concept back into the mainstream, or at least a large tributary, of evangelical conversation. They define it as "a collection of myths, traditions, symbols, narratives, and value systems—that idealizes and advocate a fusion of Christianity with American civic life...It is as ethnic and political as it is religious."[30]

Christian Nationalism forms Christians who are too much discipled by their nation's history, mythology, and governing philosophy; the story and politics of the country have become the spiritual mentor for such disciples. It combines patriotic and Christian imagery and is shocked by the idea that Jesus would object. Spiritual warfare is primarily warfare against the culture rather than against the principalities and powers who in league with the Evil One harass and oppress every people. Christian Nationalism is a hybrid that destroys the Kingdom ethos Jesus came to bring, conflating the kingdom of God with human domains.

In what can best be called a neo-fascist screed, Josh Hammer calls for a Nationalism that adapts easily into Christian Nationalism. Hammer centers "God" in one minute, "We need greater social consolidation, more meaning to our lives, and, ultimately, more God," then for jailing the enemies of his "National Conservatism" the next:

> *The only way for the American right to accomplish this, once regaining power, is to prudentially wield that power in the service of pursuing our ideal of the substantive good, and to reward friends of our just regime and punish enemies of our just regime within the confines of the rule of law.*[31]

A "just regime" requires defining both and, with Hammer a blink away from going full *Il Duce*—all in the name of making "God" central to his nationalist view of America—we can safely conclude *just* to be synonymous with "agrees with us" and *regime* with "we who are in charge." The "rule of law" will be obliterated whenever the "just regime" decides. Connect those dots and see what image lies before you.

Distinguishing between nationalism and Christian Nationalism is not the only distinction that needs to be made. Clarity between kingdoms is also needed.

> *Christian Nationalism persists despite significant biblical evidence that to be a Christian on earth is to be a member of a nation that transcends place and time. It is a nation that rejects power, oppression, the lust of the flesh, eyes, or pride of life as policy, either explicit*

> *or implicit. The "holy nation" of God's own creation is of a different order than the nations of humankind. It equates to Jesus' kingdom spanning every earthly nation, tribe, tongue, and people. The ethics of this kingdom-nation are set by its King, not by human monarchs striving to gain wealth, keep power, or establish historical remembrance. The power of this Kingdom is the power of the gospel of Christ.*[32]

Far from disconnecting from the world, those Christians who view their citizenship in heaven (Philippians 3:20) are able to live to the fullest on earth. We can serve those around us because our lives are hidden with Christ in God (Colossians 3:3); we are thus freed from nationalist impulses that otherize some bearers of the *Imago Dei*. We are free from worldly concerns centering on ourselves, but we are not freed from earthly concerns of our neighbors—wherever they might live.

Once loosed from the pseudo-biblical framework of Christian Nationalism, we can give our full attention to biblical discipleship rather than hanging so many hopes in the basket of political machinations. We return to and embrace the ethics of God's kingdom instead of those of the kingdoms of men: the lust of the fle h, the lust of the eyes, and the pride of life. Jesus' wilderness temptation to receive all the kingdoms of the world in exchange for bowing to Satan is recognized as a temptation to sin, rather than the opportunity of a lifetime.

Essay 7

Tsundoku

> *"[A] successful printed book is a stone dropped in water, its message rippling outwards to hundreds, thousands, millions."*[33]
>
> ~John Man

Question: How many books is too many?

Answer: The half has never yet been told.

I am, in the language of Japan, a practitioner of *tsundoku,* the habit (I prefer *art*) of buying books and stacking them up, or buying more books than you can ever read.[34] Book buying is my only hobby. I do not golf. I rarely attend sporting events. I have no stamp collection; no walls filled with Star Wars or Doctor Who figures. I b y books.

To be clear, I am not a book *collector*, *per se*. I don't scout out rare books, I don't shop online for volumes signed by the Pilgrims, Benjamin Franklin, or Queen Elizabeth. Although my wife and I have learned to decorate using books, my primary activity is in the buying.

Now, before someone stops the presses, let me quickly clarify: I buy very few new books. I'm not laying out $30 or $35 every Tuesday on the latest new release; that's a once- or twice-yearly endeavor for this *tsundoku* practitioner. No, my preferred venues for purchases are used bookstores (brick and mortar or online), thrift stores, and garage sales—in that order.

A used bookstore is one of the closest things to heaven on earth I've yet found. The best one near us is about 20 miles away: McKay's Used Books. Impeccably organized, well stocked, and consistently fair-pricing, for the cost of the aforementioned new hardback one can leave with 5–10 used volumes. Thrift stores like Goodwill or community-based versions have fewer good choices, but the prices are generally outstanding: $1–2 per book. Garage sales are hit-or-miss, but when someone is letting go of their hardbacks for 50 cents, it's hard to be attracted by the old sweatshirts on the next table.

If you are not a buyer of books in the practice I'm describing, perhaps this seems like too many pages of fool's errands. I get it.

Not really, I don't. I've always loved books. I read all 52 of the *Hardy Boys* series available when I was in fourth and fifth grade and however many *Alfred Hitchcock and the Three Investigators* books were to be found in Clayton County, Georgia.

In addition to years of accumulated theology books from serving as a pastor, my library contains dozens of books on writing; scores on history and biography; forty or more on food, farming, and chefs' memoirs; a few dozen specifially on the Palestinian/Israeli conflict; African-American history; fiction, and more

To be transparent, I'm not talking about e-books. Digital books are fine if you like that kind of thing. *Convenience* is an appropriate word for carrying around fifty books in a device smaller than a grocery mailer; but books are for placing on shelves, or lying on chairs, or stacking on tables, or throwing on the backseat. They aren't for swiping like midnight social media doomscrolling. A book owner should be able to pick it up and feel the heft or lack thereof, wondering how a 350-page hardback can weigh less than a 250-page paperback. Are the pages white or creme? Even or deckle edges?[35] What kind of font was used? How does the layout look?

What about the cover? Despite the old saw, you can, very often, judge a book by it. Cover design is an art—or disaster movie—all its own. Covers go through trends like other things. When the trend is bad, you see a slew of awful-looking books over the course of a few months. When the trend is good…I don't know. Trends don't make good covers; good art does. A book need not cost a fortune, be leather-bound, and smell like a freshly oiled bomber jacket to be beautiful.

I have a growing set of P.G. Wodehouse books from the same publisher, Overlook. The title-fonts match, the design matches, each has a different colored band on the spine, and the front covers feature original cartoons of Jeeves, Mr Blandings, and sundry other characters. They look authentically beautiful on the shelf. One academic book about the role of religion in rural areas in the 1950s is entitled *Baptized in the Soil* and has a captivating photo of a farm with a white-frame church just beyond a green garden on the cover. The stark silver-on-black simplicity of Matthew Martens' *Reforming Criminal*

Justice: A Christian Proposal is eye-catching as is the near opposite black-on-white front cover of Megan Phelps-Roper's *Unfollow*, her memoir of growing up in then leaving Westboro Baptist Church. Who can forget the behatted, cigarette-smoking J. Robert Oppenheimer haunting the cover of Kai Bird and Martin Sherwin's *American Prometheus*? How could Tish Harrison Warren's *Liturgy of the Ordinary: Sacred Practices in Everyday Life* be enhanced before being opened? By an unfini hed peanut butter and jelly sandwich on the cover, of course.

I love cleverly named books, and writers writing about writing have given us many. There's Karen Elisabeth Gordon's *The Transitive Vampire* and *The Well-Tempered Sentence*. I particularly like *Lapsing into a Comma* (Bill Walsh), *The Forest for the Trees* (Betsy Lerner), *Sin and Syntax* (Constance Hale), and *Origin of the Specious* (Patricia T. O'Conner). I smile thinking of Arthur Plotnik's writer's guide homage to legendary authors Strunk and White: *Spunk & Bite*. Food writers have creative juices beyond the kitchen, evidenced by Jeffr y Steingarten's *It Must Have Been Something I Ate*, along with John T. Edge's *The Potlikker Papers* and Edward Lee's *Buttermilk Graffiti*.

So, what about the reading and *tsundoku*? Of course. "Readers have the amazing opportunity to participate in humanity's ongoing conversation."[36] Readers develop critical thinking skills (as long as they aren't in a silo'd media ecosystem), learn about other cultures and places, develop theologically, and become educated outside formal paths. Reading may simply bring the pleasure of a good story, a fin ly constructed sentence, a well-turned phrase, or a twisty ending.

Reading as many books as possible is good, but it isn't the only point. Having a selection to choose from is an important reason I buy. "What about your local library?" a well-meaning reader is probably asking themselves. Well, I have a hyper-local library.

Libraries are great if you are just looking for another book, but thousands of random volumes there are of no interest to me. My personal library has books that are already curated. At some past point, these books interested me enough to buy them, so I have shelves of books at the ready for selection. Why go to the library wondering as I wander, when I can go to my offic and find volumes that already grabbed my attention?

So, buy some books. Stack them by your bed, on the coffee table, in the bathroom. Put one in your car. Or two. Be on the lookout for clearance tables, library sales, church yard sales, and used bookstores. Buy more than you can read.

But, don't you dare dog-ear those pages. That's a mortal sin.

Essay 8

The Poor You Have with You Always

The Year of Our Lord 2016

As muddled theology follows Joel Osteen, when the subject of helping the poor arises some well-meaning person interjects "The poor you always have with you." It is often inserted into conversation like a wannabe theological mic-drop, typically impressing only the one who says it.

This verse fragment—for indeed that's what it is—is found *in toto* in the gospels of Matthew (26:11), Mark (14:7), and John (12:8). The all-important context is the woman who anointed the feet of Jesus with her costly perfume, worth approximately a year's salary. Those sharing the meal with Jesus were incensed about the incense, waving away the woman's brave and contrite act of worship with their legalistic assertion it might have been sold as a fundraiser for the poor.

If that dinner was like the average church dinner, more money sat secure in the money bags of the cynics than the woman could have spilled on the feet of the Savior in another whole lifetime. Criticism being the bloodsport it is, they harangued her for the sacrifice

It is in the face of this spectacle Jesus spoke a couple of sentences, a stinging rebuke to the legalists, an incredible solace to the "dirty" woman washing his feet. If we did not have the gospel record, we might be led to think Jesus said, "The poor you always have with you," as a detached commentary of the downside of capitalism.

That, however, is not what Jesus said, or at least not all of it. From Mark's gospel we have the scene and Jesus' full response:

> *Then Jesus said, 'Leave her alone. Why are you bothering her? She has done a noble thing for Me. You always have the poor with you, and you can do what is good for them whenever you want, but you do not always have Me. (14:7)*

It seems reasonable to conclude Jesus was not saying, "You're never going to solve poverty, so concentrate on the gospel." It seems clear he meant in that instant honoring Him was the right thing to do, and using the perfume was the right kind of offering to give. Jesus juxtaposes his imminent departure with the ongoing presence of the poor. *"Honor Me now,"* He says, *"because you can do good to the poor whenever you want to."*

Jesus' response does not get us off the hook; rather, it sets the hook firml .

It is possible Jesus is quoting scripture in His response. Deuteronomy 15:11 says, "For there will never cease to be poor people in the land; that is why I am commanding you, 'You must willingly open your hand to your afflicte and poor brother in your land.'"

Bringing Jesus into a conversation about the poor to avoid helping the poor is a remarkably dull strategy.

There is a place to discuss how any society handles its poor citizens. We are not, after all, ancient Israel. It does seem, however, if the collective societal conscience is to be informed by followers of Jesus, we should demonstrate the attitude toward the poor he had. At the very least the conversation should include, "How can we best do good?" "Are unjust laws a problem?" "Is waste an issue?" "Is our pride an issue?"

One option we do not seem to be given is: doing nothing. As Brian Fikkert and Steve Corbett write in their influential volume *When Helping Hurts*,

> We believe that the coexistence of agonizing poverty and unprecedented wealth–even just within the household of faith–is an affront to the gospel. You see, what is at stake is not just the well-being of poor people–as important as that is–but rather the very authenticity of the church's witness to the transforming power of the kingdom of God. Hence, the North American church should have a profound sense of urgency to spend ourselves "in behalf of the hungry and satisfy the needs of the oppressed" (Isa. 58:10).[37]

Perhaps this is why, when Paul defended his calling before the Galatians (2:10), after recounting his meeting with the Apostles (including their blessing on his ministry to the

Gentiles), he ended with this simple request, "They asked only that we would remember the poor, which I made every effort to d ."

It is impossible to honestly read the Bible without concluding, from Old and New Testaments, that God bears witness to himself as his people help those who have little by way of worldly possessions.

Those of us in the West live in complex times with inter-relationships between disagreeable countries, ongoing racial conflicts, seemingly intractable cultural differences, challenging economic issues, and the like. But, one issue is not hard to understand: followers of Jesus should be concerned about, and engaged in, helping the poor. That one is easy.

It isn't a word.

Yes, a lot of people use it. Yes, at some point if not already, the good folks at Merriam-Webster and Oxford will succumb to mob pressure and add it to their dictionaries, declaring it a perfectly reputable word with a part of speech, definition, usage examples, and a history of development.

They will be wrong, so don't believe them. It isn't a word.

It really isn't.

So, stop saying it.[38]

Essay 10

One Christ Follower Considers the Afghanistan Papers

The Year of Our Lord 2019

"Never think that war, no matter how necessary, no matter how justified, is not a crime."

~Ernest Hemingway[39]

Yesterday, the Washington Post published "At War With The Truth,"[40] the result of a three-year effort aimed at gaining access to a trove of documents related to our 18-year-long-and-counting Afghanistan War. The documents number "more than 2,000 pages of previously unpublished notes of interviews with people who played a direct role in the war, from generals and diplomats to aid workers and Afghan official " As with the Pentagon Papers and the Vietnam War, The Post reveals private statements conflicting with public ones from the United States government and military, demonstrating an ongoing, intentional misleading of the American public. Through the administrations of George W. Bush, Barack Obama, and early into the Trump years, warfi hting strategies were fl wed, and enormous sums of money were wasted exporting democracy, or attempting it. Corruption was endemic, wrong-headed attempts to quash the opium trade made it more productive than ever, all the while claiming to the public and the press that "progress" was/is being made.

"John Sopko, the head of the federal agency that conducted the interviews, acknowledged to The Post that the documents show 'the American people have constantly been lied to.'" Well, there's a statement.

The Special Inspector General for Afghanistan Reconstruction (SIGAR) conducted over 400 interviews and used other government information before publishing seven Lessons Learned reports from 2016 to today. [As of late 2024 these reports now number in the dozens.][41]

The article is fascinating and frustrating in what it reveals, such as throwing money into a non-modern country without a hint of how to effect vely spend it. "One unidentified contractor told government interviewers he was expected to dole out $3 million daily for projects in a single Afghan district roughly the size of a U.S. county. He once asked a visiting congressman whether the lawmaker could responsibly spend that kind of money back home: "He said hell no. 'Well, sir, that's what you just obligated us to spend and I'm doing it for communities that live in mud huts with no windows.'" Don't read past it: $3,000,000 a *day*.

The article reports rampant corruption, inadequate progress for Afghan military and police force effect veness, and, echoing Vietnam, attempts to manipulate public opinion. Bad news was already known when Donald Rumsfeld, still Secretary of Defense, blessed the hiding of a 40-page negative report according to the story. Rumsfeld has been out of the offic since 2006 and the war continues. As does putting lipstick on the pig. One senior NSC officia said in 2016, "The metrics were always manipulated for the duration of the war."

Perhaps the conscience-challenging piece of information should be the estimated 43,000 Afghan civilians killed so far—nearly 1,000 more than the aggregate number of Taliban and other insurgent fi hters killed. Both are well behind the 64,000+ Afghan security forces deaths.

The open publication of secret documents produced for the benefit of the government but hidden from the public is necessary for a self-governing people. We cannot correct what we do not know. It is too easy for any government—including that of the United States—to hide information from us—the ones responsible for holding them accountable. When the government can lie and obfuscate about the effect veness of war, government official can keep from paying the piper on Election Day. In most such instances "the government" is the president—whether Kennedy, Johnson, Nixon, Bush, Obama, or Trump—and the administration he heads. Historically, whistleblowers, press reports, congressional hearings, veterans, or some combination reveal calamitous decisions and corrosive behaviors that keep wars hot and the public, simultaneously, unsurprisingly, in the cold.

What should followers of Jesus think about these things?

Some would argue merely that "war is hell," that things happen in war that cannot be controlled. This much is true. People go crazy. Massacres occur outside the rules of engagement. Innocents are killed accidentally and on purpose. Bombs go awry. Airplanes malfunction. Positions are overrun. Orders are misunderstood. Sound judgment is lost at some times, while it remains in others.

There is a fog of war. What we should have learned since the coining of that phrase is the fog envelopes those on the ground, those at HQ, those at the Pentagon, those in Congress, those on 5th Avenue, and those on Main Street. At many turns, we do not see clearly nor understand fully. Manipulation and deception can go unchecked for years; it has on more than one occasion.

Prosecution of a modern war that lasts eighteen years in a single, distant, undeveloped country depends on the suspension of focus from the people back home. I would argue what's happening in Afghanistan does not cross the mind of the average American, more than once or twice in forever. It isn't the focus of mealtime discussion, prayer groups, knitting circles, book clubs, or sermons. American veterans of Afghanistan, generally, are neither vilified like their Vietnam compatriots nor canonized as World War Two's Greatest Generation. After nearly two decades of active fi hting, former NFL player Pat Tillman remains not only the most famous person to have died in the War on

Terror, but, aside from a few generals, possibly the most famous person to have served in it.

This should lead to more pause, not less, for Christians. The Holy Spirit and scripture, not adrenaline or nationalistic pride, should guide our thinking. What others forget we should remember: eternity never ends and war sends thousands of people into it unprepared.

Former Supreme Allied Commander, U.S. President, and President of NATO, Dwight D. Eisenhower, famously warned of a "military industrial-complex" that would come to dominate our society, even to the soul and spirit. Today, his prescient words are equally appreciated, ignored, or unknown. Followers of Jesus, however, should know. We should know because we serve a Savior who refused a standing army or the political overthrow of Rome; a Savior who said, "My kingdom is not of this world," who healed the detached ear of an enemy, who forgave the ones who were at that moment crucifying him. The kingdom of God was not established by terrestrial warfare nor will it be expanded by such. A bloodthirsty Christian is quite the moronic oxymoron.

Eisenhower was not only right on the spiritual implications of the military-industrial complex. He was right to warn about its economic, materialistic foundation. Speaking to the nation on January 17, 1961, he said:

Our military organization today bears little relation to that known by any of my predecessors in peacetime, or indeed by the fighting men of World War II or Korea.

Until the latest of our world conflicts, the United States had no armaments industry. American makers of plowshares could, with time and as required, make swords as well. But now we can no longer risk emergency improvisation of national defense; we have been compelled to create a permanent armaments industry of vast proportions. Added to this, three and a half million men and women are directly engaged in the defense establishment. We annually spend on military security more than the net income of all United States corporations.

This conjunction of an immense military establishment and a large arms industry is new in the American experience. The total influence — economic, political, even spiritual — is felt in every city, every State house, every office of the Federal government. We recognize the imperative need for this development. Yet we must not fail to comprehend its grave implications. Our toil, resources and livelihood are all involved; so is the very structure of our society.

> *In the councils of government, we must guard against the acquisition of unwarranted influence, whether sought or unsought, by the military-industrial complex. The potential for the disastrous rise of misplaced power exists and will persist.*
>
> *We must never let the weight of this combination endanger our liberties or democratic processes. We should take nothing for granted. Only an alert and knowledgeable citizenry can compel the proper meshing of the huge industrial and military machinery of defense with our peaceful methods and goals, so that security and liberty may prosper together.*

Ike's concern was the influence of what we commonly call "the defense industry"—a more benign term than military-industrial complex—would become so economically interwoven in American society, that our lives and our livelihoods would come to depend on it, with "grave" and "disastrous" results. One such result is that those of us who are seated in the heavenlies with Christ have come not only to trust in horses and chariots rather than the name of the Lord our God, but hold fervently to a troubling theological substitution as if Jesus Christ himself designed the first Patriot missile battery and deployed it in Galilee. An economy that elevates the military-industrial complex is an economy that depends on war. An economy that depends on war is an economy at odds with the Kingdom.

Reading the signs of the times is more than trying to discern when Christ might return. I would argue a fixation on the timing of Christ's return can blind end-times enthusiasts from other important realities to which Christians should turn their time, energy, and search for truth. How war is prosecuted should be of the utmost concern to Christians. Of those 42,000 Afghan civilians who have been killed over eighteen years, how many of them died without Christ? That question is far more important than the bottom lines and stock valuations of arms manufacturers like Northrop Grumman, General Dynamics, Raytheon, or Lockheed Martin. If Christ is to be believed, the destiny of our "enemies" supersedes our retirement portfolios. Paul was willing to be banished to eternal hell and damnation if his unbelieving countrymen would come to faith in Christ. Jesus implored us to pray for those who hate and persecute us.

Of all people on earth who should resist the urge to embrace earthly, imperial goals they should be followers of Jesus. It was, after all, a political empire that put Jesus to death at the insistence of a religious power structure. "You take him and kill him yourselves. I don't find anything wrong in him," said the Roman procurator tasked with quelling Jewish revolts. Pontius Pilate couldn't be troubled to defend Jesus to the end, so he allowed the lamb to be slaughtered. What a Friend We Have in Empire is not the tune that made the hymnal.

The marriage of the American Civil Religion with Christianity birthed a child which, under most lighting, more resembles the former than the latter. A 23 and Me of twenty-firs century American Evangelicalism might reveal ancestral DNA we'd rather not have known and the presence of siblings we'd rather ignore. In all cases followers of Jesus should cast a jaundiced eye toward anything that smacks of hubris, empire, and worldly power, remembering the prince of this world still wars against us through principalities and powers, and that these principalities and powers work to erect and maintain the shiny towers of our endless Babylons. Our city is the Jerusalem that is above from where the King reigns over his kingdom not made with human hands, nor maintained by human legislation, nor expanded by military might. May we demand more of a our government than a bland disinterest in war as long as we have the freedom to go shopping.

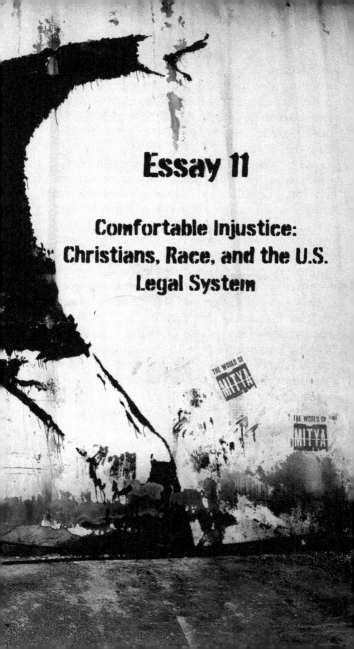

Essay 11

Comfortable Injustice: Christians, Race, and the U.S. Legal System

The Year of Our Lord 2012

Justice is turned back, and righteousness stands far off; For truth has stumbled in the public square, and honesty cannot enter.

~Isaiah 59:14

Vindicate me, God, and champion my cause against an unfaithful nation; rescue me from the deceitful and unjust person.

~Psalm 43:1

But let justice flow like water, and righteousness, like an unfailing stream.

~Amos 5:24

The subject of justice has enjoyed a resurgence of interest in the Christian community of late. I think this is rightfully so. For so long, filled with the hope of Christ's immediate return, we tended to ignore our neighbors asleep on the sidewalk heating grate in favor of watching the next installment of *A Thief in the Night*. Those who gave compassion to the poor–and demanded the same from others–were often derided as "liberal" or promoting a works-based salvation in which societal reform *is* the gospel. We rejoiced that Jesus was with the two or three of us gathered in his name, but seemed to forget he also promised to meet us in prison or when he was naked *as long as we ministered to him in those cases.* Forming a holy huddle of prayer after Sunday night church is one thing; taking the stranger Jesus into our home is quite another (Matthew 7:34-46).

Owing much to the heartbeat of young believers who have proclaimed that being the light of the world means being in the world enough to light it, there has been a renewal of interest in stopping injustice wherever it occurs. It is now easier to convince believers who were formerly on the sidelines to stand against sex traÃĀkers, corporate exploitation of third-world workers, government undercutting of a national economy (suffered by Haiti, for instance), or to become involved in adoption movements. Injustice now arouses our anger. Even when we do not know exactly how to act we are, at least, moved viscerally to pray. We are concerned and we often express it online, on the phone, or in person.

Despite recent advances, one area where issues of justice have a hard time building a fan base concerns the injustice of the American "justice" system. Many of us were taught, via Romans 13, to be strong supporters of our government. Thus, excepting overtly anti-biblical atrocities like abortion-on-demand, we are hesitant to critique the state—sometimes far too hesitant. (That hesitancy is quickly cast aside if the party opposing our cherished beliefs controls Congress or the White House. In such cases critique is all some Christians know.)

As it now stands in the United States, the most consistent, the most embedded, the most troublesome injustice *is* our justice system. It has become a perpetual motion machine of search, arrest, cajole, convict, and imprison. Adam Gopnik writes[42]:

> *Mass incarceration on a scale almost unexampled in human history is a fundamental fact of our country today—perhaps the fundamental fact, as slavery was* **the** *fundamental fact of 1850. In truth, there are more black men in the grip of the criminal-justice system—in prison, on probation, or on parole—than were in slavery then. Over all, there are now more people under 'correctional supervision' in America— more than six million—than were in the Gulag Archipelago under Stalin at its height. That city of the confined and the controlled, Lockuptown, is now the second largest in the United States.* (**Emphasis in original.**)

Mass incarceration resulting from perverted justice, like the flu, is endemic. It is just the way of things.

In her troubling book, *The New Jim Crow*, Michelle Alexander writes,[43]

> *In two short decades, between 1980 and 2000, the number of people incarcerated in our nation's prisons and*

> jails soared from roughly 300,000 to more than 2 million. By the end of 2007, more than 7 million Americans—or one in every 31 adults—were behind bars, on probation, or on parole.

Constitutional attorney John W. Whitehead notes[44]:

> Consider this: despite the fact that violent crime in America has been on the decline, the nation's incarceration rate has tripled since 1980. Approximately 13 million people are introduced to American jails in any given year. Incredibly, more than six million people are under "correctional supervision" in America, meaning that one in fifty Americans are working their way through the prison system, either as inmates, or while on parole or probation. According to the Federal Bureau of Prisons, the majority of those being held in federal prisons are convicted of drug offenses—namely, marijuana. Presently, one out of every 100 Americans is serving time behind bars.

How we treat those we imprison starts with the lengths we are willing to go to imprison them in the first place. Since the 1970s that length has stretched like taffy on a hot day. This is especially true when the incarceration of African-Americans is concerned.

In *Race, Incarceration and American Values* the authors write:

> Between 1980 and 1997 the number of people incarcerated for nonviolent offenses tripled, and the number of people incarcerated for drug offenses increased by a factor of eleven. Indeed, the criminal-justice researcher Alfred Blumstein has argued that **none of the growth in incarceration between 1980 and 1996 can be attributed to more crime**...As of 2000, thirty-three states had abolished limited parole (up from seventeen in 1980), twenty-four states had introduced three strikes laws (up from zero), and forty states had introduced truth-in-sentencing laws (up from three). The vast majority of **these changes occurred in the 1990's as crime rates fell. (Emphasis added.)**[45]

Racial bias in the legal system is pervasive, from arrest to execution.

> In 2008, four out of five arrests were for mere possession of drugs, one-half of those for marijuana. Due to selective enforcement, those imprisoned are primarily minorities.
>
> **While there is no evidence to support that African-Americans use drugs at a higher rate than white Americans,**

> **and although they make up only 12.6 percent of the general population, African-Americans account for 37 percent of total drug arrests annually and 56 percent of incarcerations.** *As Georgetown University law Professor David Cole put it, were whites being arrested at the same rate as blacks, "We would almost certainly see this as an urgent national calamity, and demand a collective investment of public resources to forestall so many going to prison."*[46] **(Emphasis added.)**

Regardless of one's position on the War on Drugs, it exists and federal laws drive it. Thus, it is unjust to search, arrest, prosecute, and imprison members of one race to a greater degree when the evidence suggests equal violations across races.

And, while sentencing disparities have been recognized for many years they remain. A 2019 paper found:

> Even with recent reforms, more than two million Americans remain behind bars of jails or prisons. Black men and women are imprisoned at roughly six times the rate of their white counterparts.[47]

Studies that examine death-penalty cases have generally found that:

- In the vast majority of cases, if the murder victim is white, the defendant is more likely to receive a death sentence;

- In a few jurisdictions, notably the federal system, minority defendants (especially blacks) are more likely to receive a death sentence.[48]

A multi-decade study by the US General Accounting Office fou

> *'a pattern of evidence indicating racial disparities in the charging, sentencing, and imposition of the death penalty.' The study concluded that a defendant was several times more likely to be sentenced to death if the murder victim was white. This has been confirmed by the findings of many other studies that, holding all other factors constant, the single most reliable predictor of whether someone will be sentenced to death is the race of the victim. From charging decisions to plea bargaining to jury sentencing, African-Americans are treated more harshly when they are defendants, and their lives are accorded less value when they are victims.*[49]

Findings by the federal government and academic researchers demonstrate our judicial process counts white lives as more valuable than African-American lives. This is racism by definition and it's baked into the criminal justice system.

Christians in the United States cannot claim to hate racism while supporting an unjust legal system that exercises racial oppression. Selective application of the law and biased prosecution of accused are not justice. We cannot claim to love justice when, at the federal, state, and local levels, all manner of corruption and unfair dealing makes it difficul for certain segments of the population to get a good lawyer, have a fair trial, or expect balanced sentencing.

In addition to the well-known admonition to "pursue justice and justice alone" in Deuteronomy 16:20, scripture warns not to rob the poor of justice (Exodus 23:6); not to pervert justice (Leviticus 19:15); not to deny justice to a resident alien, orphan, or widow (Deuteronomy 27:19); not to deny justice to an innocent person (Proverbs 18:5); and that the heart far removed from justice is hardened (Isaiah 46:12).

Are you looking to live a righteous life? That path corresponds to the path of justice. As Solomon wrote, "Then you will understand righteousness, justice, and integrity—every good path (Proverbs 2:9). He personifies wisdom when saying "I walk in the way of righteousness, along the paths of justice (8:20). The scriptures are replete with God's concern for justice. Christians would do well to recover God's passion for it and let his Word shape our understanding of how righteousness should look in a criminal justice system rather than reflecting political tough-on-crime talk or TV legal dramas. Since no state is infallible, and since egregious violations of justice saturate the historical record, it behooves the people of God to pursue justice even at the cost of our personal comfort or political in-group acceptance.

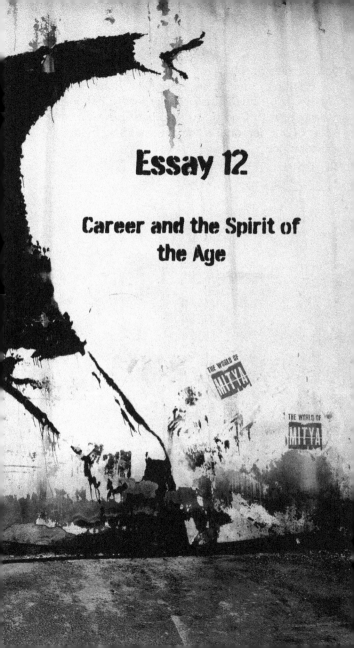

The Year of Our Lord 2022

What is life if not an unending string of changes? Infancy changes into childhood, childhood into adolescence, adolescence into adulthood. Food preferences change. Styles, music, hobbies, routines. Virtually everything is subject to some degree of change.

Enter the career.

My father worked for a major automotive manufacturer for thirty years, retiring before he was old enough to collect social security. My father-in-law retired from a multinational production company, also after about thirty years. The lion's share of their working years was given to one employer.

I did not follow in their footsteps. Nor do I now.

For the fourth time in four years I will commence on a different employment path—not counting the 5-week stint as an Amazon delivery driver at the end of 2018. And since those few words were published, I've been through two more jobs, both sales-oriented, neither of which can I wrangle enough income to make a living. My goal of getting a full-time job that I enjoy, providing benefits and matching 401(k), seems beyond my grasp...and beyond that of many people on LinkedIn.

We are likely a few years away from the body of academic work examining how the capitalist economic system shapes the Christian disciple.

It is neither feasible nor possible to think—with even a modicum of reality—that cultural pressure and influence inherent in world-bending economic power does not influence how those of us in the West—and in the United States particularly—perceive and experience our entire lives. As the authors of *Freakonomics* note, "If morality represents how we would like the world to work, then economics represents how it actually does work."[50] It is the actual world Christian disciples inhabit rather than an ideal world, and we are not immune from its discipleship. It is a type of worldliness.

Walter Benjamin was a German-Jewish cultural critic, media theorist, and essayist in the early 20th century. Part of his critique of capitalism was its religious nature. "A religion may be discerned in capitalism—that is to say, capitalism serves essentially to allay the same anxieties, torments, and disturbances to which the so-called religions offered answers."[51] It can, for the deceived Christian, become a way of life, a type of faith, that displaces the walk of faith in God that he calls us to.

Christian discipleship is always a journey through a darkened world; growth at the edge of contaminated soil; sailing against the winds of the age. There are many metaphors; these are but a few that are obvious. We exchange truth, make self-adjustments to survive the seas of life, sometimes not realizing how much we adjusted course away from the Kingdom.

There's an old saw I heard many years ago about how windy it is in Nebraska: One time the wind stopped blowing and everyone fell down. When you are so accustomed to leaning into the wind, when your whole life develops resisting the wind every day, everywhere, and all the time, you forget why you are leaning forward, striving just to walk. It isn't supernatural; it's just the way it is. When the wind dies for an instant, you face-plant before you can adjust. It's the same as the fi h asking, "What's water?" That which surrounds us (our parents, grandparents, and additional ancestral generations) is simply our existence.

It is the same way following Jesus in an economic system that overshadows every aspect of life: how we work, where we work, when we work, how we feel about work, how others perceive our work, the value we generate from work (for ourselves and others), when we get to quit work, how much we make, how much we have, how much we save, how much we invest, how much we owe and to whom we owe it. Christians' understanding of these, in the American context to be sure, is immeasurably informed by The Man and the Machine, likely more than by the Spirit and the Word. We have embraced a counterfeit abundant life and do not notice the stranger in our arms.

I am not an economist, nor am I much more than a scant theologian. But in my older years, while learning more about living the Christian *life*, it has become clear it is more than reading the Bible more and praying more; that coming out from among them and being separate has to do with more than sexual mores and condemning the most convenient sins. It includes recognizing, rejecting, and standing against the principalities and powers behind the systems we often dismiss as innocuous, but, in reality, pile heavy burdens on our backs that neither we nor our ancestors could bear.

Essay 13

The Bearable Whiteness of Being

The Year of Our Lord 2014

The first time I became truly self-aware of being a member of the white race (not just a white guy) was when I visited Kenya, Africa in 1995. I was in the country for two weeks for a mission trip.[52] My team had been dropped off in a town to do evangelism, but two members were being driven to another area for reasons I don't remember.

So, I stood on the side of the road in this small town south of Nairobi with only black skin in every direction; except mine. The object of some curiosity, I wondered if it was how a black man in 1950s south Georgia might have felt. Minus the racial slurs and potential lynching, of course. I was not merely white; I was the sole white. And did I ever stick out. It was pretty clear white folks did not visit the town often.

Often as an adult, I've reflected on a time in junior high school when a black friend named Willie had been accused of some infraction and was heading to the offic to visit Mr. Rogers, our main principal. In protest, Willie turned to me and said, "Marty, tell'em I didn't start it!" I've wondered whether Willie was hoping my social standing as a white guy would lend support to his own testimony which was quite evidently not being believed. (For the record, I did not see who started it and said as much.)

Over the last couple of years, reflecting on how biblical justice looks in our world on a practical level, I have had occasions to write about racial issues. The subject has no lack of fodder, much of it heartbreaking. I have written about unjust prosecution, incarceration for profit, out-of-control police action, slavery, Jim Crow, the "War" on drugs, and the convict-lease system. Every such effort was met with appreciation from African-American friends, and sometimes those who are mere acquaintances. When I have written about violence against women I have been thanked for speaking out. When getting advice on this article I was encouraged to move forward. A friend said, "It's only when white men step into the fray that anything will really change." I didn't take him to mean only white men say things that are important; that's clearly not the case. On the contrary, it's absurd that so many people only hear what black people have been saying forever after some white person they respect says the same thing. I understood him to mean because white men have a certain standing in American society—pretty much as a birthright—change comes more quickly when we finally step up

The contours of biblical justice reveal a responsibility for those in power to stand for the oppressed. As there is an inherent power that comes from being a white male in America. My voice matters, as does yours if you are a white American male. This is especially true when we lift it on behalf of those who have no voice, or whose voice is ignored, marginalized, or suppressed. Our opinion matters, especially when it challenges the accepted narrative. My weight, such as it is, matters, especially when thrown alongside those being pushed around. I must speak when society affords those like me the privilege of being heard without having to ask for it.

It is my responsibility, my opportunity, and, yes, my privilege.

I am concerned less with whether my congressman, senator, the press, or the president ever hear my voice, but I am very concerned that those who are oppressed know that someone else is speaking on their behalf. As another friend recently said, "In a situation of oppression, to not side with the oppressed is to side with the oppressors. Moreover, in my view, God is on the side of the oppressed. His love requires it and Jesus reveals it. So, to fail to side with the oppressed is to fail to side with Jesus."

The events of the last few days in Ferguson, Missouri, have unfolded in slow, agonizing motion. Young black man shot and killed, mourning, demonstration, rioting, overbearing police action, more demonstrations, better police action, great community response.

Why did so few white followers of Jesus raise the roof when a young black man—in the middle of a neighborhood street, unarmed, surrendering, already shot once or twice—was shot to death in broad daylight by one sworn to protect and to serve?

Why did so many white followers of Jesus finally start raising their voices and sharing multiple stories on social media when rioting and looting erupted from a demonstration against the police force responsible for the shooting?

Clearly, for many, the site of potato chips burning at a convenience store evokes more emotion than a dead black teenager. While looting and rioting are frustrating, the fact remains that Quick Trip can repair, restock, and rebuild if so desired. Michael Brown is gone forever.

Many white folks roll their eyes when the likes of Jesse Jackson or Al Sharpton show up, grab a mic, and start making accusations. Fair enough. White folks do not like all white people with a mic, either; some are completely embarrassing, to be honest. But, is a lack of appreciation for Jackson or Sharpton enough reason for me to not respond immediately to the death of another unarmed black man at the hands of law enforcement? I cannot conceive of how or why that should be.

Let's assume for one moment that there exists some not-yet-released evidence that paints Brown in the worst light. What if Brown was guilty of theft, rather than only suspected of it, just before the shooting? Then he should have been arrested, cuffed, then put in jail pending his arraignment. He should not have been shot to death in the middle of a neighborhood street.[53]

Most white American men have no frame of reference for why Greg Howard can write "America is not for black people",[54] or why Jordan Lebeau can write "Because most Americans are cowards."[55] The typical white American male response would be, "Love it or leave it" without even a second thought as to why it is possible for an entire segment of the population to feel the way these two black men, and many others, feel.

By virtue of our status in society, white men have a responsibility to stand in the gap, to jump into the fray on the side of the voiceless, the dispossessed, the unjustly treated, the unfairly charged, the abused, and the exploited. Not only because we are white, nor merely because we are men. I am not advocating racial or gender superiority. Instead, because we are the majority and by virtue of that, there are injustices that will remain entrenched if we do not speak out. Proverbs 31:8, 9 says, "Speak up for those who have no voice, for the justice of all who are dispossessed. Speak up, judge righteously, and defend the cause of the oppressed and needy." We cannot simply pull these verses out every January for Sanctity of Life Sunday. Truly, if we believe in the sanctity of life we should be speaking up for communities like Ferguson, Missouri, and black men who are even today doing nothing wrong other than being black men in the United States.

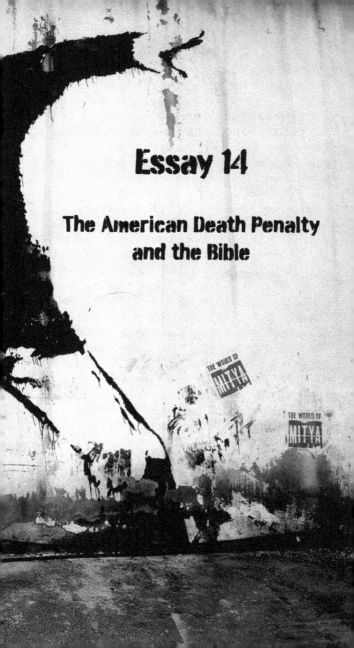

> *"The death penalty is the criminal justice system at its worst."*
>
> ~Ernie Lewis[56]

> *"There can be no equal justice where the kind of trial a man gets depends on the amount of money he has."*
>
> ~Justice Hugo Black[57]

Like many reading these pages, I grew up believing "an eye for an eye and a tooth for a tooth" was intended as the ground of modern judicial punishment. I also grew up believing that death at the hands of the state, aka 'capital punishment' was biblically sound based on several other Old Testament passages. The Bible does not merely back into capital punishment, but insists on it at times. For instance:

Genesis 9:6, "Whoever sheds human blood, by humans his blood will be shed, for God made humans in his image."

Exodus 21:12, "Whoever strikes a person so that he dies must be put to death."

Exodus 21:15, "Whoever strikes his father or his mother must be put to death."

Exodus 22:19, "Whoever has sexual intercourse with an animal must be put to death."

Leviticus 20:10, "If a man commits adultery with a married woman—if he commits adultery with his neighbor's wife—both the adulterer and the adulteress must be put to death."

Leviticus 20:27, "A man or a woman who is a medium or a spiritist must be put to death; they are to be stoned; their death is their own fault."

Leviticus 24:16, "Whoever blasphemes the name of the Lord must be put to death; the whole community is to stone him. If he blasphemes the Name, he is to be put to death, whether the resident alien or the native."

In the New Testament, we find in Romans 13: "Let everyone submit to the governing authorities, since there is no authority except from God, and the authorities that exist are instituted by God...if you do wrong, be afraid, because [the authority, ie, the state] does not carry the sword for no reason. For it is God's servant, an avenger that brings wrath on the one who does wrong" (1, 4). To be sure, the way of Christ emphasizes love, to the point of allowing someone to slap both cheeks; give up both a shirt and coat; and, if compelled into carrying some soldier's pack, go for two miles instead of one. These teachings from Jesus contrasted with the Old Testament's "eye for an eye."

So, the scripture does not blanket-condemn the power of the state to put *some* lawbreakers to death. Thus, I do not oppose the death penalty on purely moral grounds. That is, I cannot say the death penalty is always at all times and in all places a moral evil. If it was, scripture would condemn it like it condemns adultery and covetousness. If capital punishment is ontologically equivalent to murder—which is clearly condemned in scripture—it seems likely stoning a person to death as punishment for a crime would be prohibited as well. But it isn't.

Or is it?

It would be overstatement to place capital punishment in the category of "overarching scriptural themes" like the holiness of God, the goodness of God, the mission of God, or the justice of God. But it is in this last category, the justice of God, where we must pause to ask: *If the death penalty is carried out in ways that violate the justice of God, does it become a moral evil in that society?*

The study of scripture and society has brought me a "yes" to that question. So while I cannot say capital punishment as "a thing" is morally wrong, I can say capital punishment as "our thing" most certainly is.

Many exonerations over many decades have led even the most casual observer to conclude something is out of whack. A 2014 study concluded that "a conservative estimate" of innocent people under sentence of death is 4.1%.[58] In some cases, their attorney made a mistake; in some cases, police planted evidence; in some cases, the prosecuting attorneys hid exculpatory evidence; in some cases, witnesses changed their testimony; and in some cases, DNA evidence years after a conviction proved the convicted prisoner didn't commit the rape or murder.

Because the courts consider "adequate assistance" by a defense lawyer to be a hairbreadth above present and breathing, some accused get less-than-stellar defense. The standard is so low that

> *in 2001...the First Circuit Court Of Appeals openly debated whether to affirm a death-penalty decision where the lawyer, Joe Frank Cannon, had slept through significant parts of his client's case...Nine judges of the Fifth Circuit agreed to overturn the death penalty decision and grant [the convicted] a new trial, but not without five dissenters, two of whom took issue with how much of the trial it was permissible to sleep through and still be adversarial.*[59]

So, Your Honor, effective counsel can be determined by how much shut-eye the defense attorney gets during a trial that determines whether Mr or Ms Defendant gets the needle, the noose, the gas, Old Sparky, or walks free. Got it.

If ineffective counsel is not bad enough, ineffective justices ought to ensure all capital punishment is mothballed. Two Supreme Court justices, the late Antonin Scalia and Clarence Thomas, wrote that neither the U.S. Constitution nor American jurisprudence give an innocent person the opportunity to be heard in court based on new evidence: "There is no basis in text, tradition, or even in contemporary practice...for finding in the Constitution a right to demand judicial consideration of newly discovered evidence of innocence brought forward after conviction."[60]

As the prophet wrote, "Justice is turned back, and righteousness stands far off. For truth has stumbled in the public square, and honesty cannot enter" (Isaiah 59:14).

Among the many questions justice requires us to confront are these: *How many are unjustly put to death because new evidence came too late?* Similarly, *How many years of life are stolen because a conviction tainted by the intentional injustice of a police officer or prosecutor—a person seeking career advancement or a higher case closure rate?* And, *"How many have been executed or are languishing on death row because of unjust laws?"* Finally, *"Aren't the disparities between white people sentenced to death and black people sentenced to death a raging symptom of injustice?"*

The angles from which the US justice system could be examined are many. Prosecutorial misconduct? In *For the People: A Story of Justice and Power*, defense attorney turned district attorney of Philadelphia, Pennsylvania, Larry Krasner references a former DA in his city.

> *"The prosecutorial threat to seek death was cynically used to coerce guilty pleas for sentences of life in jail with no chance of parole, even when the circumstances of a case and the defendant's history did not support a death sentence. Everyone in the system knew that a jury picked*

> *for a death penalty case, all of whose members have confirmed they could impose a death sentence, was more likely to convict during the guilt phase than a jury that includes people who are opposed to the death penalty. So some prosecutors' pursuit of the death penalty was really about fixing the trial on guilt by getting a jury biased toward guilt during the guilt phase."*[61]

In other words, prosecutors rejected jurors who opposed the death penalty, creating a jury already predisposed to vote for the death penalty. Not hard to imagine a bias toward the death penalty would affect a bias toward a "guilty" verdict. Not only do some prosecutors game the system on jury selection, they withhold evidence that could benefit the accused before the jury is ever selected. One study by Chicago Tribune found 11,000 cases of prosecutorial misconduct between 1963 and 1999, including 381 homicide convictions overturned, 67 of which saw the defendants sentenced to death.[62]

Bias in conviction and sentencing? Regarding the death penalty

> *there is compelling evidence that the race of both victim and offender is a key element in the determination of which convicted murders receive the death penalty. In a review of twenty-eight studies examining these issues, the*

> *General Accounting Office concluded that, 'In 82 percent of the studies, race of the victims was found to influence the likelihood of being charged with capital murder.'*[63]

Those charged with murdering white victims got harsher treatment than those charged with murdering black victims. Are black people worth less or do we just treat them so when they are murdered? Does it have anything to do with charges brought by prosecutors who, as recently as 2015, were comprised of 95% white people?[64]

If the system is so messed up the death penalty can be wrongfully given to hundreds of people, where is the justice? It is no longer a *justice system*; it's just a *system*. And it's hard to beat the system.

Christians need to give strong thought to whether we can support the death penalty. The principles of justice laid out in scripture provide us enough light to see the pursuit of justice requires us to remove our approval from a system that so often perverts it.

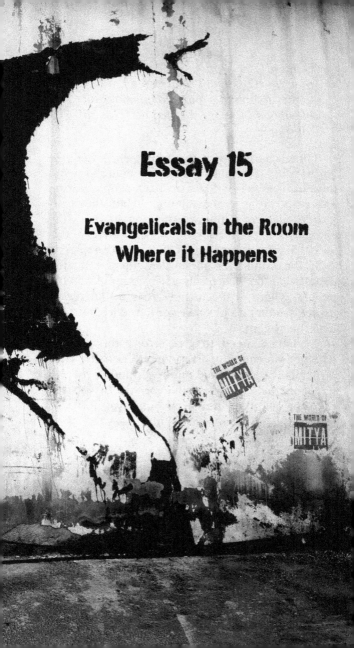

Essay 15

Evangelicals in the Room Where it Happens

The Year of Our Lord 2020

"I wanna be in the room where it happens."

~Aaron Burr in *Hamilton*[65]

Few things are more necessary and more avoided than reading history especially when that history critiques a movement you hold dear. Over the last few years, such works have served as historical colonoscopies for 20th-century American evangelicalism. And like a physical colonoscopy, they are inconvenient, irritating, and revealing. But, perhaps, even lifesaving.

Kevin Kruse's *One Nation Under God: How Corporate America Invented Christian America* provides an evangelical-historical critique based on secular business interests. He argues that modern "religious identity" in America was formed in the 1930s and early 40s in opposition to FDR's New Deal policies.

> *Decades before Eisenhower's inaugural prayers, corporate titans enlisted conservative clergymen in an effort to promote new political arguments embodied in the phrase "freedom under God"...[T]his new ideology was designed to defeat the state power its architects feared most—not the Soviet regime in Moscow, but Franklin D.*

> Roosevelt's New Deal administration in Washington. With ample funding from major corporations, prominent industrialists, and business lobbies such as the National Association of Manufacturers and the US Chamber of Commerce in the 1930s and 1940s, these new evangelists for free enterprise promoted a vision best characterized as "Christian libertarianism."[66]

While Kruse's work is not a critique of evangelicalism *per se*, that movement's embrace of American capitalism and free enterprise aligns with Kruse's broader study. One need only survey the warnings from pastors about "socialism" in the 2020 election to see it in action.

In *Jesus and John Wayne: How White Evangelicals Corrupted a Faith and Fractured a Nation*, Calvin University's Kristin Kobes Du Mez describes how evangelicals adopted among other things military postures and a prominent patriotism that "would help them overcome their reputation as extremists and their marginal status"[67]. In the shadow of Vietnam, authors from Jerry Falwell to John Price to Hal Lindsey connected revival or renewal to reinvigorated American military might. In his book *Listen, America!* "Falwell lamented that the United States was 'no longer the military might of the word.'" Price saw that "only when America 'comes to its senses' and 'repents of its sins and turns to God' would its military position be restored." Lindsey's *The 1980's: Countdown to Armageddon* treated rearmament as "a religious requirement."[68] Fortunately, as with most prophecy books, the countdown timer slowed considerably. Now 40 years on, no one can accurately project how many ticks are left; not John Hagee, not David Jeremiah, no, not even the angels of heaven.

Helping evangelicals overcome "marginal status" is another way of saying "they wanted to be in the room where it happens." But did they sell their city down the river in exchange? Augustine has entered the chat.

In the introduction to Aaron Griffi 's *God's Law and Order: The Politics of Punishment in Evangelical America* is a section that tied together loose ends in my mind. In the aftermath of the Leopold and Loeb murder trials in 1924, Americans wanted more law and order around two points: recognition that increases in crime reflected increasing secularization and that punitive state action was needed to address the increase. Griffith write

> *Political leaders drew on these shared sensibilities as they built national support for the expansion of tougher law enforcement efforts. This broad consensus meant that future religious movements that want to exert widespread cultural influence would need to take crime seriously.*[69]

Griffit shows the religious groups who wanted *broad* cultural influence would have to adopt a *specific position* on law and order. Admission to the room is predicated on knowing the password. Over time we can track a trend: specific political positions adopted for access in one generation become the gospel in the next. Specific positions adopted for continued access in the second generation become the gospel in the next. So that, several generations down the line "gospel fid lity" is far more than Jesus dead, buried, risen, and coming again, reigning King of a kingdom of light; it's a compilation of gospel truth and political deal-making, nearly indistinguishable in the hearts or minds of the adherents. In the end, if someone disagrees on a political point, they have not merely reached a different con lusion: they've denied the gospel.

Such syncretism might well inflame Paul to write Second Colossians from his eternal dwelling.

Desiring to be in the room where it happens does not at the outset require a naked, drooling lust for power. It need not, because power is its own corrupter. It is a short walk through an inviting door from *desiring to be in the room* to *needing to be;* political power-seeking often being a mutation of cultural influence. When any group—evangelicals included—is given access to the room, a seat at the table, a pass to the corridors of power, they leave the room with an expectation that the door will remain open, the seat available, and the corridor swept and well-lit. And if that means bowing to principalities and powers in barter for kingdoms of the world, just throw in a Johnson Amendment promise to seal the deal.[70]

In American history, evangelicals have adopted certain power postures and political positions, perhaps with a desire, as Griffit notes, for sincere cultural influence but ending with greater alignment with the political party granting entrance into the room. Being lights in this world requires no Hollywood-esque, pseudo-spiritual gimmickry, a production of The Truman Show Goes to Church. It requires Jesus.

We never see Jesus seeking to be in the room where it happened. He was called and content to live his life and manage his ministry with everyday folks in towns and despised folks on the margins. When he finally gained an audience with Rome, it was because he'd been accused and arrested, not because he was seeking a new tax code. In metaphor: Jesus is his Church, Pilate is American politics, and the religious leaders are, well, the religious leaders. Choose you this day whom you will serve and all that.

Jesus stood before both Pilate and Herod lacking earthly power yet having all power. He put no trust in horses, chariots, lawyers, or judges. Jesus was never willing to trade his kingdom authority for temporal position, not even to stay his execution. Jesus did not need to be in the room where it happened because he owned the building; it is ever thus. Our willingness to trade away spiritual power and biblical witness for political soup and a moldy baguette is a sorrowful example of Paul's warning against claiming a type of godliness but denying the power of it.[71]

In 2024, as this was being edited for publication, Donald Trump was elected president for the second time and for the third election cycle, he's captured 80% of the Evangelical vote. He did this partly by promising "You're gonna have more power than ever." Can a president offer spiritual power? Can he empower God's people to walk in the light, to overcome sinful habits, to love God with all our heart, soul, mind, and strength? No. The power an earthly leader can provide is political power, the very kind that disinterested the Savior. Have we forgotten that Jesus has given us the Kingdom?[72] That he turned his back on the kingdoms of the world? What are we doing?

American Christians often look back at the early church and marvel at its spiritual power, forgetting it had no political power, and its cultural influence was limited to the people personally touched by their witness. When plague hit Rome and Christians ministered to the oft-abandoned dying, they were still viewed as a fringe religious group; their influence was hardly broad. They didn't consult with Caesar. No one was in the room where it happened. But they had been in a room: an upper room, where the Spirit of God empowered them for the task they were assigned.

My point is not that Christians should ignore politics altogether, refuse to vote, or merely throw darts as disaffected grumblers. My point is that the embrace of worldly power comes at a cost, a cost that is often unrecognized at the outset, until, like generations of a recessive family trait suddenly provides a redhead after twenty black and browns, the result becomes clear. But for the Church, the trait isn't merely a hair color; it is a disease. Thus infected by worldly power, we become unable or unwilling to give it up, so we can return to the source of true power.

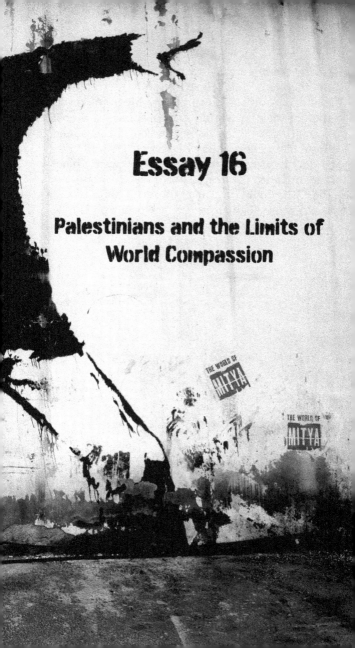

Essay 16

Palestinians and the Limits of World Compassion

On October 7, 2023, armed Hamas militants accompanied by fighters from the Al Aqsa Martyrs Brigade breached the retaining wall separating the Gaza Strip from Israel proper. They went on a rampage that ended with more than one thousand killed and 240 stolen away hostage to hidden places inside Gaza. Given the well-developed and extensive tunnel network under the Strip, many were likely hidden underground.

The world was rightly aghast at the barbarism. Entire families were killed. Concertgoers at a festival were slaughtered. Men, women, and children were shot. Video taken by members of Hamas showed celebration over the deaths. It was disgusting and appalling. It was, as many noted, the largest mass killing of Jews since the Holocaust.

It was not long before Israel prepared retaliation, with the full support of a U.S. budget as bottomless as Chili's chips and salsa. It is an unwritten rule in modern American politics that Israel gets what it wants. Partly, but not solely, because the current Israeli Prime Minister, Benjamin Netanyahu, is a genius at manipulating the American body politick. He has spoken to more joint houses of Congress than any world leader in history. Virtually all Republicans and virtually all Democrats support Israel. Virtually no Republicans and virtually no Democrats rebuke her. The few who do are ignored. It is pretty much a one-way street of blessing from this world superpower to the "only democracy in the Middle East," as we are assured Israel is.

Netanyahu's stated objective was the eradication of Hamas, to which this writer found no objection. Although Hamas is a political party within Palestinian life, it isn't recognized as one by the world at large. It doesn't even have the full support of Palestinians in Gaza. Other Israeli politicians were not as coy. One suggested turning Gaza into a parking lot, while another suggested pushing all Palestinians into the Mediterranean. A retired general wanted to kill all the residents of Gaza. Many across Israeli society, in and out of government, in and out of the military, view all Palestinians as terrorists, and responded accordingly.

Given the nature of urban warfare—and Gaza, one of the most densely populated areas on earth, is nothing if not urban—a ground invasion was anticipated by many. Removing terrorists from labyrinthian tunnels would require innumerable troops committed to rounding blind corners, risking booby traps, chasing shadow and rumor from street to street and door to door.

So, Israel opted for an air campaign to "soften things up." Bomb after bomb. Missile after missile. It was not long before video emerged of collapsed buildings, ostensibly to kill one Hamas member hiding in one room of a refugee camp. Entire families from children to their grandparents all killed in single bombings. Apartment buildings destroyed. Homes destroyed.

A mere three months into the war, Israel's ordinance on the Gaza Strip outpaced military attacks on Germany during World War 2.

> *Between 1942 and 1945, the allies attacked 51 major German cities and towns, destroying about 40-50% of their urban areas, said Robert Pape, a U.S. military historian. Pape said this amounted to 10% of buildings across Germany, compared to over 33% across Gaza, a densely populated territory of just 140 square miles (360 square kilometers).*
>
> *"Gaza is one of the most intense civilian punishment campaigns in history," said Pape. "It now sits comfortably in the top quartile of the most devastating bombing campaigns ever."*[73]

By November 2023, Israel had equaled the destructive power of two nuclear bombs.[74] By April 2024, Israel had dropped an estimated 70,000 tons of explosives, more than were dropped on London by the Germans, and on Hamburg and Dresden by the Allies. This does not include bulldozing of homes and buildings, a tactic routinely used by Israel in the occupied territories.[75] So many buildings have been destroyed, the Shelter Cluster, an international coalition of aid providers, recently estimated it could take forty years to rebuild Gaza.[76]

The members of Hamas and Al Aqsa Brigades who remained in Gaza are to this day continuing to fi ht with their store of homemade rockets and grenades, the latter of which are typically placed directly on tank turrets by hand. The Palestinians have no actual army, navy, or air force, so once hostilities break out it's pretty much death by the barrel until some sort of truce is reached. Since Hamas has returned only some of the hostages after more than a year, the fi hting continues.

The recent history of military campaigns against Gaza, generally enticed by Hamas and Palestinian militant groups, have happened in 2008–09, 2012, 2014, and 2021. In each and every instance the number of Palestinian civilian dead far exceeds the number of Israeli dead, both military and civilian. Criticism of Israel's military occupation of the West Bank and the multi-year control of supplies into and out of Gaza continue to arrive from all corners of the political world, from Israel's allies to her enemies. One not versed on the conflict might assume most or all of the criticism comes from Muslims, militants, or academics. Such is not the case. Jews from many lands including Israel have long been vocal in their opposition to the occupation. Organizations like B'Tselem (The Israeli Information Center for Human Rights in the Occupied Territories), Breaking the Silence (an organization of former IDF members who speak out against Israeli military abuses in the occupied territories), and Jewish Voice for Peace hope and work to end the violence.

A full exploration of the conflict is beyond the scope of this essay or, frankly, any group of essays. I have dozens of books in my library on this history alone. It's been addressed by Jews, Gentiles, Israelis, Palestinians, the International Criminal Court, the United Nations, and a myriad of politicians globally. So I don't hope to solve the issue.

I write to raise the question: *why do Palestinians matter so little?* As of this writing, more than 42,000 are known to have died in Gaza, mostly women, the elderly, and children. More children have been made amputees since October 2023 than in any other conflict in human history, at one point ten per day lost one or both legs not counting those who lost arms and hands.[77] There are almost certainly tens of thousands of bodies buried and decaying under the miles of rubble from north to south in the strip. Survivors are constantly ordered from one area to another so further bombing can take place. In many instances, the "another" is a place that also gets bombed.

Although the Christian population of Gaza is practically non-existent, a few of Jesus' sheep wander those dusty paths. The Christian population of the West Bank is also small, about 1%. The percentage of Christians in Israel is also small, a reported 1.9%, with about 3/4 of them Arab Christians. Since there is a Palestinian church, no matter how small, why in the face of ongoing hostilities do American churches hardly, if ever, pray for them? For every mention of Palestinian Christians, you'll find a million or more bumper stickers, memes, or church prayer lists with "Pray for Israel" or "Pray for the Peace of Jerusalem." I'm all for praying for Israel, but perhaps a few prayers for Israel's government and their military not to view Palestinian children as terrorists should also be directed to the throne.

I've been blessed to travel to Israel twice. I did the obligatory "Holy Land tour" each time. I'm not going to diminish it: it is meaningful to walk where Jesus walked; to stand by the Sea of Galilee and imagine the great catch of fi h; to visit the place he was born and where he might have given his first sermon; to look across from the Mount of Olives to Jerusalem; to stand on the Mount of Ascension. It is deep, as Bono once mused, to stand where the sins of the whole world were paid for.

Palestinian Christians acknowledge this. They know the depth of spiritual meaning; they live there. The birthplace of Jesus is in the West Bank. They see Christian pilgrims from all over the world in such a hurry they run where Jesus walked. They drive past their homes, schools, and places of business in tour buses doing their window photography on their unbothered way to the Church of the Nativity. This obliviousness to Palestinian suffering in preference for buildings and walls gave rise to the phrase, "Don't forget the Living Stones."

Palestinian Christians told me, "We feel like the forgotten part of the body of Christ." They understand evangelical infatuation with Israel, but do not understand how so many Christians can ignore the suffering of other Christians. When the Hebrews author wrote, "Remember those who are suffering as though you were sufferin ," I don't think it was an exercise in phrase-turning. Prayer for those who have never heard is great, but can we not also offer up petitions on behalf of those who have heard, who have accepted the message by faith, and who are sufferin , if not directly for that faith, directly in it? What part of Christ's body should feel forgotten?

The difference in the way Palestinian Christians view their situation and the way most American evangelicals view it is stark. Mind-bogglingly so. Palestinian Christians call their situation a "military occupation." American evangelicals call it "security for Israel." American evangelicals rejoice over the embassy being moved to Jerusalem. Palestinian Christians are leery of what the politics behind it will mean for them. Palestinian Christians tell of PTSD symptoms from frequent IDF military incursions, tear gas, and rubber bullets. American evangelicals complain about imagined persecution.

Palestinian pastor and scholar Alex Awad writes,

> *Despite the abundant information available about the conflict, Palestinians consistently feel that our story is, in the end, marginalized. We believe that the Israeli perspective virtually saturates public discourse, leaving us voiceless, misunderstood, and stereotyped. We do not have the political, military, or financial strength of our oppressors, who often use their power to sway world opinion and to conceal or alter the historical facts behind our suffering.*[78]

Palestinian Christians are not listless in their spiritual growth nor resigned to their sufferin . They plant churches. They have a Bible college. They contribute to theological studies. They write books. They minister the gospel in the name of Jesus. "If we really want to understand the Bible's message, it is of utmost importance to listen to Palestine's native people. Their suffering under occupation, their aspiration for liberation, their struggles and hopes are relevant to exegesis."[79]

If American Christians ever do face genuine sufferin , rather than a little poison ivy-like discomfort, we will do well to learn from our Palestinian brothers and sisters who have suffered faithfully for decades. If suffering is to come our way, I pray we are remembered far better than we have remembered.

Essay 17

Abortion

Over the last 50+ years there was probably no greater call to arms in American politics than to be for or against abortion. [80]That sentence is quite milquetoast describing the real divide. These, being more emotive, are also more telling:

Are you for or against the right to kill children in the womb?

Are you for or against a woman's right to control her own body?

Are you for or against doctors being able to provide medical care for their patients who are mothers-to-be even if that means ending the life of the fetus?

Are you for or against state legislatures run by non-medical personnel deciding laws that regulate the procedure even when the life of the mother is endangered?

Do you believe abortion is taking an innocent in any and all circumstances?

Do you believe in some exceptions, such as pregnancy resultant from rape or incest, or the mother's life or health is at substantial risk?

During the years after the Supreme Court's *Dobbs* decision reversed a previous Court's *Roe v Wade* decision, a polarizing issue went to polar extremes. "Red States," dominated by Conservative legislatures, passed ever-tighter restrictions on abortion accessibility. "Blue States," dominated by Liberal legislatures, passed new abortion-access laws or strengthened existing laws. Citizens in Blue and Red states secured abortion rights via state constitutional challenges, aka, ballot measures. Within the first year, according to the Allen Guttmacher Institute, 77 provisions that would protect or expand access to abortions were enacted; 50 provisions were enacted that would restrict access.[81] Abortion laws became and remain a free-for-all, not unlike the years before *Roe*.

The 2024 election cycle saw Joe Biden vowing to retain abortion access, Kamala Harris celebrating abortion access with a promise, were she to be elected president, to sign any Roe-like legislation that crossed her desk. Donald Trump left it alone, claimed victory from the Supreme Court in *Dobbs*, and insisted against every shred of evidence that an overturned *Roe* is what everyone—including Liberals—wanted. He chose not to make abortion part of his campaign. Other than a few hardcore pro-lifers, most Republicans supported Trump's approach.

Now, for the first time since Jerry Falwell's Moral Majority, we might be entering a period when immigration, the economy, climate change, or some other arguable issue—anything but abortion—takes center stage.

This is—to say the least for Christians who printed pro-life bumper stickers and voter guides, produced t-shirts and marches—odd.

I come from a long pro-life history. When I was around 15- or 16-years-old, I encouraged my church to host a showing of *The Silent Scream*, a pro-life film. It showed a recorded ultrasound of an abortion taking place. At some point during the procedure, the fetus opens its mouth in what narrator and former abortionist, Bernard Nathanson, called a "silent scream." The entire church was moved to murmurs, sounds of surprise, then silence of its own.[82]

Not long after, our church began sidewalk protests at one of the busiest abortion clinics in the state. I was at the first protest and attended numerous others. I wrote letters to our congresspeople; to the newspaper; wherever. I voted only for pro-life candidates for many years, even at the local level, believing even the dog catcher couldn't do a good job unless he opposed abortion.

The only quibble I can remember in my long-held pro-life convictions is when I shifted from the historically conservative rape, incest, and life of the mother exceptions to what would now be called an "abolition" view where no exceptions are allowed. For reasons I no longer remember, I returned reasonably quickly to the "exceptions" position and remain there.

Since Dobbs, another thing has happened that has not gotten much press: longtime pro-lifers have become pro-choice. Not by the millions, surely, but a lot. Many are women, even Christian women. Evangelicals for Harris, even if they did not embrace her position on the issue, were willing to deprioritize it for one election. My suspicion is the Donald Trump effect. Trump's appointment of three very conservative Supreme Court justices led to *Dobbs*. *Dobbs* led to such restrictions in some states that hospitals and medical personnel are not rendering timely help for pregnant women in distress. The abortion issue pushed a shift from "protect the unborn" to "why don't people care if women die?"

Christians are quick to pull up Psalm 139:13–16 and Jeremiah 1:4 to oppose abortion. The former reads, "For it was you who formed my inward parts; you knit me together in my mother's womb. I praise you, for I am fearfully and wonderfully made. Wonderful are your works; that I know very well. My frame was not hidden from you, when I was being made in secret, intricately woven in the depths of the earth. Your eyes beheld my unformed substance. In your book were written all the days that were formed for me, when none of them as yet exists." (NRSVue)

The latter, "Now the word of the LORD came to me saying, 'Before I formed you in the womb I knew you, and before you were born I consecrated you; I appointed you a prophet to the nations.'" (NRSVue)

It is important to note in each of these cases, the men writing were asking for help in the moment (in the case of David) and receiving assurance of a life-calling (in the case of Jeremiah). In neither of the cases are the writers pondering the nature of pre-born life. David is saying, "I can't get away from you no matter where I go. Heaven? You're there. The grave? You're there, too. You know what I'm going to say before I say it. Not only did you knit me in my mother's womb, you knew me before I was ever in my mother's womb."

Similarly, with Jeremiah, God was preparing his new prophet for what would turn into a torturous assignment. "Jeremiah, I'll put the words in your mouth to judge nations. You'll speak what I tell you; you aren't a boy. At your word, kingdoms will be plucked up or pulled down, destroyed or overthrown, given the opportunity to build and to plant. And in case you think I just dreamed this up, nope. I planned this before I even formed you in the womb. I appointed you before your momma and daddy had any idea about you."[83]

These verses have been used for decades by Christians including me to demonstrate the value of the unborn. I believe such is taught indirectly in these passages, but recently the question comes to mind: At what post-birth age does that value expire? Or, to put it another way, *where in scripture does it teach unborn life is always to be valued more than the life of the mother-to-be?* If we insist no abortions can be allowed for any reason, the underlying position must be that unborn life is *always* more valuable than born life, including the lives of women and specifi ally those who are pregnant via rape, incest, or their life or health is at risk. For the abolitionist or those who restrict abortion without or nearly without exception, the woman has little intrinsic value except as a birth canal.

Consider for a moment the victim of incest, a 12, 14, or 15-year-old girl, impregnated by a father, brother, or uncle. Ashamed of their circumstance and likely unable to report to the police, she's slut-shamed for the crime committed against her. She has to live a lie about how she got pregnant, or tell the truth, then who knows? Incest Aware says

> The effects of incest are severe. The majority of survivors victimized by someone they know (79%) experience substantial harm that affects their work, school, and emotional state. For many incest survivors, <u>sexual victimization continues in adulthood</u>, as child abuse survivors are substantially more likely than non-survivors to be revictimized as adults. As <u>ACE research</u> shows, traumatic childhood events such as incest are closely linked to many physical and mental health problems, substance abuse, and education and job struggles. Survivors are <u>10 times more likely</u> to attempt suicide than those who haven't.[84]

The common argument against abortion availability for incest victims (and rape victims) is, "Two wrongs don't make a right." Fair enough. Then which of the traumas in the paragraph above are *right*? Is it the emotional damage? The additional victimization? Suicide attempts? Which of those is right?

Now, how does a 14-year-old keeping and delivering the child of her father make the incest right?

It doesn't.

At this point someone will stand and object that, "Incest accounts for only about .5% of all abortions. Abortion shouldn't be legal for that little amount." To which I answer, "That's why they are called exceptions, not rules. A mere .5% is the reason to have an exception."

The same type of argument can be made for rape. The fact is, some women choose to keep children conceived of rape, but some do not or at least desire not to. Laws in many states force women to relive their rape trauma over and over before an abortion can be obtained. A hospital rape exam; reporting to law enforcement; and facing the possibility their non-convicted[85] rapist, who, by claiming parental rights, can be in her life indefinit ly. And with the same argument, the same question: *If two wrongs don't make a right, which of the above is right?* We cannot simply wave away women, who are also made in the image of God, as if their existence does not matter.

It used to be the "life or health of the mother" was the exceptional exception. But nowadays it isn't as easy as all that. Not only because the laws in some states vaguely allow abortions in such cases, but because hospitals and medical personnel are left uncertain whether some procedures violate new laws. How close to maternal death is close enough to warrant help? Should we let her bleed a little more, for a little longer?

The truth is, the mother-to-be is created in the image of God. She likely has a spouse or a significant other. She might have others at home that call her "mommy" for whom she prepares breakfast and dinner and perhaps holds down a job, contributing to, if not providing, the family income. Is her life not important? Is she expected to die, likely taking her unborn with her, for a human law, but not a biblical one, the devalues her life in favor of another?

As this essay was in composition, four women in Idaho got a day in court challenging the state's abortion ban. Each of them had been carrying children they wanted to keep, but were advised to have an abortion for their own sake. In each of the four cases, the unborn child would not only likely die in utero or be stillborn, but could possibly kill the mother. In one case, the woman's future fertility was at risk. In her opening statement, plaintiff' attorney Gail Deady said:

> *The state appears to believe that the lives and health of living, breathing, pregnant Idahoans, people's sisters, mothers, wives, friends are inherently less valuable than a developing fetus or embryo. And that continued pregnancy and childbirth must be forced in all situations and at all costs, except when both the woman and the developing pregnancy would be lost without an abortion.*[86]

The exceptions are incredibly important to a holistic Christian witness and biblical fidlity. We must consider the value of the women involved, not merely the unborn. Laws that threaten a woman's life or future pregnancies to protect a fetus until its inevitable death are unjust.

But in every pregnancy there is an unborn human being involved; this is indisputable. It is to the unborn we now turn.

The history of Christianity is not complete unless we acknowledge how Christians have, through the millennia, valued human life from the womb to old-age. Christians understand and embrace the *imago Dei* ("image of God") in every person. Marred though the image might be due to sin, the image remains and it should be respected, and, whenever possible, protected.

Proverbs 31 tells us to "speak for those who cannot speak for themselves." This has application outside the unborn, to be sure—immigrants, racial oppression, those abused by the legal system—but it can hardly be argued the unborn have a voice apart from the already-born who will care for them.

Until the beginning of the 3rd century, adult Roman men held the life and death of their newborn children at a whim. "[H]e might expose his new-born child to perish of cold and hunger or be devoured by dogs on one of the public refuse dumps."[87] The early Christians rescued Roman infants from the dumps. Some eventually started the first orphanages. They believed something distinct from the surrounding culture: children have value. They need not be contributing workers in the economy, warriors in the army, or teachers in the academy. Little boys and girls splashing in the rain are *imago Dei*. No Roman *paterfamilias* had authority from God to say, "Throw it out," when Jesus says, "Let them come to me."

A recent conversation with an unbelieving friend turned to abortion. She asked, "What about fetuses that have no hope of survival? Those whose lives aren't compatible with life outside the womb?" It's a fair question and one not devoid of concern. My response was, "It's compatible with life now. Why should we abort in the womb simply because compatibility will not exist outside the womb?" I wasn't intending to be flippant; my pastoral years put me in touch with people in that very situation. Friendships have done the same. Many women deliver knowing their child will not long survive, so they love that malformed infant as well as they can during the brief earthly sojourn. That is recognizing the *imago Dei*.

Similarly, countries that allow targeting Down's Syndrome children for abortion have completely lost the plot. As of 2017, some European nations were seeing almost no Down's births at all. Choosing to end pregnancy because the developing fetus is deemed inferior to society at large is eugenics and nothing less. I'm not making a slippery-slope argument; once humans decide—based on arbitrary social customs or bad science—which lives are valuable, who deserves life and who does not, history shows a broadening, not narrowing, of those deemed unfit for life. In *War Against the Weak*, Edwin Black chronicles decades-long American eugenics movement in the early- to mid-1900s. He writes of the hundreds of thousands of affected ind viduals:

> Selected because of their ancestry, national origin, race or religion, they were forcibly sterilized, wrongly committed to mental institutions... prohibited from marrying, and sometimes even unmarried by state bureaucrats...Specious intelligence tests, colloquially known as IQ tests, were invented to justify incarceration of a group labeled "feebleminded"... Mandatory sterilization laws were enacted in some twenty-seven states to prevent targeted individuals from reproducing more of their kind.[88]

Boys *and* girls were sterilized; in some cases, all the siblings in a family. Anyone lacking blond haired, blue-eyed Nordic features could be targeted. All across America, from sea to shining sea, "poor urban dwellers and rural 'white trash'... Blacks, Jews, Mexicans, Native Americans" were victimized by sterilization, imprisonment, and commitment to mental institutions. Still, eugenics was a global initiative, eventually making its way to Germany where it informed Nazi social policy, leading to the Holocaust.[89]

How we think about human life matters to God. He really did know David and Jeremiah's innermost physical development. He really used Christianity to elevate women, showing they had equal value as men. When he organized a mission to rescue humanity from the curse and enslavement of sin, he sent his Son, conceived through the Spirit, and carried by a Middle Eastern Jewish girl. Jesus' identification with humanity began where virtually every human begins: inside the womb of a woman.

Abortion is not a great solution to difficul problems. Women who are rape victims and decide to keep the baby are incalculably brave. A mom-to-be who decides to deliver her child who has died in utero, preferring the natural course over an artificially terminated pregnancy, should receive all the support family, friends, and medicine can provide, as should an incest or rape victim who decides for adoption. Abortion is a decision with its own set of outcomes, not all positive. It's an oft-abused procedure that exists in a fallen world. Yet, we live in a country where Jewish and Muslim religious beliefs do not always preclude abortion and where Christian thought is not 100% aligned even among Christians. Shall the State have authority to force victims of sexual violence to carry their abuser's child against her will? Should it legislate such strictures as to leave women whose health or being is at risk no option other than that risk?

Perhaps in these situations—rape, incest, and life or health of the mother being at substantial risk—the decision should be between the woman and God, rather than the woman and the State. In the end, God will judge her actions toward her pregnancy. And ours toward her.

Endnotes

ESSAY 1

[1] — "What do 'fine-tuning' and the 'multiverse' say about God?" *BioLogos.com*. (November 20, 2023). https://biologos.org/common-questions/what-do-fine-tuning-and-the-multiverse-say-about-god
[2] — 1 John 2:16 (NRSVue)
[3] — 1 John 2:15 (NRSVue)
[4] — Stott, John R.W. *The Letters of John, Tyndale New Testament Commentaries*, rev. ed. (Leicester: InterVarsity Press, 1990), 104.
[5] — Ibid, 105, *emphasis in original*.
[6] — See Galatians 5:16–21 and Colossians 3:5–9.

ESSAY 2

[7] — Bacote, Vincent E. *The Political Disciple: A Theology of Public Life*. (Grand Rapids: Zondervan, 2015), 46.
[8] — Schiess, Kaitlyn. *The Liturgy of Politics: Spiritual Formation for the Sake of our Neighbor*. (Downers Grove: InterVarsity Press, 2020), 17.
[9] — Abraham Kuyper, quoted in Koyzis, David T. *Citizenship Without Illusions: A Christian Guide to Political Engagement*. (Downers Grove: InterVarsity Press, 2024), 72.
[10] — The last "other party" president was Andrew Johnson (1865-69), a member of the National Union party.
[11] — Koyzis, p 76.

ESSAY 3

[12] — "For God So Loved Caitlyn Jenner." *Kingdom in the Midst*. (June 2, 2015). http://blog.martyduren.com/2015/06/02/god-love-bruce-caitlyn-jenner-gender-reassignment/, accessed, October 23, 2024.
[13] — "Loving the Way Jesus Loved." *Kingdom in the Midst*. (June 3, 2015). https://blog.martyduren.com/2015/06/03/loving-the-way-jesus-loved/, accessed October 23, 2024.

ESSAY 4

[14] — In *Four Thousand Weeks*, Oliver Burkeman observes, "It turns out that when people make enough money to meet their needs, they just find new things to need and new lifestyles to aspire to…As a result, they work harder and harder, and soon busyness becomes an emblem of prestige. Which is clearly completely absurd: for almost the whole of history, the entire point of being rich was not having to work so much." One biblical concept for "find[ing] new things to need" is covetousness, the religion of temporality. *Four Thousand Weeks: Time Management for Mortals.* (New York: Farrar, Straus, Giroux, 2021), 11.

[15] — Smith, James K. A. *How to Inhabit Time: Understanding the Past, Facing the Future, Living Faithfully Now.* (Grand Rapids: Brazos Press, 2022), 23.

[16] — Nagel, Thomas. *Mind & Cosmos: Why the Materialistic Neo-Darwinian Conception of Nature is Almost Certainly False.* (Oxford: OUP, 2012), 14.

ESSAY 5

[17] — Wirzba, Norman. *Food and Faith: A Theology of Eating, 2nd Ed.* (Cambridge: Cambridge University Press, 2019), 305.

[18] — Conversation with the author.

[19] — Noble, Alan. *Disruptive Witness* (Downers Grove: InterVarsity, 2022), 114.

[20] — Wood, Gaby. "Interview: Joel Salatin." *TheGuardian.com.* (January 30, 2010) https://www.theguardian.com/lifeandstyle/2010/jan/31/food-industry-environment, accessed October 23, 2024.

[21] — Street, Alan. *Subversive Meals: An Analysis of the Lord's Supper under Roman Domination during the First Century.* (Eugene, OR: Pickwick Publications, 2013), 7.

[22] — Logan, Ben. *The Land Remembers: A Story of a Farm and Its People.* (New York: Viking Press, 1975), 26.

ESSAY 6

[23] — Gellner, Ernest. *Nations and Nationalism.* (United Kingdom: Cornell University Press, 2008), 1, 42-43. Accessed October 19, 2024, https://www.google.com/books/edition/Nations_and_Nationalism/Aqidsw3SkDUC?hl=en&gbpv=0

[24] — Smith, Anthony D. *Nationalism: Theory, Ideology, History.* (Germany: Polity Press, 2013), Ebook chapter 1. https://www.google.com/books/edition/Nationalism/6_uK8_-StVIC?hl=en&gbpv=0, accessed October 19, 2024.

[25] — Wyatt, Adam. *Biblical Patriotism: An Evangelical Alternative to Nationalism*. (Denver: GCRR Press, 2021), 97–98.
[26] — Ibid, 98.
[27] — Ashford, Bruce R. "The Religious Problem with Nationalism." *BruceAshford.net*. (September 8, 2018). https://bruceashford.net/2018/the-religious-problem-with-nationalism/, accessed January 1, 2022.
[28] — Chadwick, John. "Christian Nationalism Explained: An Interview with Rutgers Professor Joseph Williams," *Rutgers School of Arts and Sciences*. (March 4, 2021.) https://sas.rutgers.edu/about/news/faculty/faculty-news-detail/religious-nationalism, accessed October 19, 2024.
[29] — Backhouse, Stephen. *Kierkegaard's Critique of Christian Nationalism*. (United Kingdom: OUP Oxford), 2011, xii. https://www.google.com/books/edition/Kierkegaard_s_Critique_of_Christian_Nati/5AFREAAAQBAJ?hl=en&gbpv=0, accessed October 19, 2024.
[30] — Mikva, Rachel S. "Christian nationalism is a threat, and not just from Capitol attackers invoking Jesus," *USAToday*. (January 31, 2021.) https://www.usatoday.com/story/opinion/2021/01/31/christian-nationalism-josh-hawley-ted-cruz-capitol-attack-column/4292193001/, accessed October 19, 2024.
[31] — Hammer, Josh. "The Only Path Forward is National Conservatism," *The American Conservative*. (November 5, 2021). https://www.theamericanconservative.com/articles/the-only-path-forward-is-national-conservatism/, accessed October 19, 2024.
[32] — Duren, Marty. "A Christian, Nationalism, and the Kingdom of God," *Kingdom in the Midst*. (November 30, 2021.) https://blog.martyduren.com/2021/11/30/a-christian-nationalism-and-the-kingdom-of-god/, accessed October 19, 2024.

ESSAY 7

[33] — John Man. *Gutenberg: How One Man Remade the World with Words*. (New York: MJF Books, 2002), 2.
[34] — tsundoku, *noun* /ˈsʌn.doʊ.kuː/, the practice of buying a lot of books and keeping them in a pile because you intend to read them but have not done so yet; also used to refer to the pile itself. https://dictionary.cambridge.org/us/dictionary/english/tsundoku
[35] — For more on deckle edges see https://bookriot.com/history-of-deckle-edges/.
[36] — Ryken, Leland and Glenda Faye Mathes. *Recovering the Lost Art of Reading: A Quest for the True, the Good, and the Beautiful*. (Wheaton: Crossway, 2021), 162.

ESSAY 8

[37] — Fikkert, Brian and Steve Corbett. *When Helping Hurts: How to Alleviate Poverty Without Hurting the Poor and Yourself.* (Chicago: Moody, 2009), 16.

ESSAY 9

[38] — I'm serious.

ESSAY 10

[39] — Quoted in Elliott, Steven. *War Story: Sometimes the Real Fight Starts After the Battle.* (Carol Stream, IL: Tyndall Momentum, 2019), 67.
[40] — Craig Whitlock. "At War with the Truth." *WashingtonPost.com.* (December 9, 2019). https://www.washingtonpost.com/graphics/2019/investigations/afghanistan-papers/afghanistan-war-confidential-documents/, accessed October 21, 2024.
[41] — Lesson Learned Reports." *Special Inspector General for Afghanistan Reconstruction.* (various) https://www.sigar.mil/lessonslearned/lessonslearnedreports/index.aspx?SSR=11&SubSSR=60&WP=Lessons%20Learned%20Reports, accessed October 21, 2024.

ESSAY 11

[42] — Gopnick, Adam. "The Caging of America." *NewYorker.com.* (January 30, 2012.) www.newyorker.com/arts/critics/atlarge/2012/01/30/120130crat_atlarge_gopnick?currentPage=all, accessed November 18, 2024.
[43] — Alexander, Michelle. *The New Jim Crow: Mass Incarceration in an Age of Colorblindness.* (New York: The New Press, 2012), 60.
[44] — Whitehead, John. "Jailing Americans for Profit: The Rise of the Prison Industrial Complex." *Rutherford.org.* (April 10, 2012.) https://www.rutherford.org/publications_resources/john_whiteheads_commentary/jailing_americans_for_profit_the_rise_of_the_prison_industrial_complex, accessed November 18, 2024.
[45] — Loury, Glenn C., Pamela Kaplan, Loïc Wacquant, Tommie Shelby. *Race, Incarceration, and American Values.* (Cambridge: MIT Press, 2008), 8, 9, 10.
[46] — Schneider, Mark and Steve Ellman. "Commentary: 40 years of War on Drugs Failure: Rethink the war-fighting model." *PalmBeachPost.com.* (June 16, 2011.) https://www.palmbeachpost.

com/story/news/2011/06/16/commentary-40-years-war-on/7468929007/, accessed November 11, 2024.

[47] — Grawert, Ames, Bryan Furst, and Cameron Kimble. "Ending Mass Incarceration: A Presidential Agenda." (January 1, 2019.) *Brennan Center for Justice*. http://www.jstor.org/stable/resrep28435, accessed November 11, 2024.

[48] — Kansal, Tushar. "Racial Disparity in Sentencing: A Review of the Literature." *The Sentencing Project*. (January 2005.) https://www.opensocietyfoundations.org/uploads/764bf150-13d8-4330-b08b-b04ae313308f/disparity.pdf, 2–3, accessed November 11, 2024.

[49] — "Death Penalty and Race." *Amnesty USA*. (updated June 26, 2023.) https://www.amnestyusa.org/issues/death-penalty/death-penalty-facts/death-penalty-and-race/, accessed November 11, 2024.

ESSAY 12

[50] — Levitt, Steven D. and Stephen J. Dubner. Freakonomics: *A Rogue Economist Explores the Hidden Side of Everything, Revised and Expanded Edition*. (New York: William Morrow, 2006). Quote at https://www.goodreads.com/book/show/1202.Freakonomics# (accessed November 15, 2024).

[51] — Clapp, Rodney. *Naming Neoliberalism: Exposing the Spirit of Our Age*. (Minneapolis: Fortress Press, 2021), 58.

ESSAY 13

[52] — For readers outside church world, a "mission trip" is a group of church members who travel to an area away from home to spread the message of Jesus Christ. Such a trip can be inside or outside the church's home country.

[53] — Even after all these years, the narrative about what happened in Ferguson remains unclear, partially due to contradictions between Officer Darren Wilson's grand jury and civil suit testimony. Wilson was not charged with a crime and the civil suit brought by Brown's parents was settled.

[54] — Howard, Greg. "America is Not for Black People," *Deadspin*. (n.d.) https://deadspin.com/america-is-not-for-black-people-1620169913/, accessed November 9, 2024.

[55] — Jordan Lebeau. "Because Most Americans Are Cowards," *medium.com*. (August 14, 2014). https://medium.com/thsppl/because-most-americans-are-cowards-1541f13487ba, accessed November 9, 2024.

ESSAY 14

[56] — Lewis, Ernie. "From the Prison to the State House." *Doing Justice to Mercy: Religion, Law, and Criminal Justice.* eds, Jonathan Rothchild, Matthew Myer Boulton, Kevin Jung (Charlottesville: University of Virginia Press, 2007), 53.

[57] — *Griffin v Illinois*, 351 U.S. 12, 19 (1956), quoted in Bach, Amy. *Ordinary Injustice: How America Holds Court.* (New York: Metropolitan Books, 2009), 271, n66.

[58] — Gross, Samuel R., Barbara O'Brien, Chen Hu, Edward H. Kennedy, "Rate of false conviction of criminal defendants who are sentenced to death," *Proceedings of the National Academy of Sciences of the United States of America* 111 no. 20 (May 20, 2014): 7230.

[59] — Bach, 54.

[60] — *Herrera v. Collins*, 506 U.S. 390, 398, 400, 417 (1993). Quoted in Martens, Matthew T. *Reforming Criminal Justice: A Christian Proposal.* (Wheaton: Crossway, 2023), 334.

[61] — Krasner, Larry. *For the People: A Story of Justice and Power.* (New York: Penguin Random House, 2021), 58.

[62] — Martens, 269. The failure of the prosecution to provide the defense with evidence that could help a defendant or is "material" to his/her guilt or punishment is called a "Brady violation" after the Supreme Court ruling in *Brady v Maryland* (Martens, 266).

[63] — Mauer, Mark. "Race, Class, and the Development of Criminal Justice Policy." *Doing Justice to Mercy: Religion Law and Criminal Justice.* Rothchild, Jonathan, Matthew Myer Boulton, Kevin Jung, eds. (Charlottesville: University of Virginia Press, 2007), 15–16.

[64] — Jones, Rick. "From the President: See No Evil: Prosecution and Unchecked Discretion," *The Champion.* (January/February 2018). https://www.nacdl.org/Article/January-February2018-FromthePresidentSeeNoEvilPros, accessed November 10, 2024.

ESSAY 15

[65] — Miranda, Lin Manuel. *Hamilton: An American Musical.* Atlantic Records, 2015, MP3.

[66] — Kruse, Kevin. *One Nation Under God: How Corporate America Invented Christian America.* (New York: Basic Books, 2015), xiv.

[67] — Du Mez, Kristin Kobes. *Jesus and John Wayne: How White Evangelicals Corrupted a Faith and Fractured a Nation.* (New York: W. W. Norton, 2020), 24.

[68] — Ibid, 111.

[69] — Griffith, Aaron. *God's Law and Order: The Politics of Punishment in Evangelical America.* (Cambridge, MA: Harvard University Press), 9.

[70] — The Johnson Amendment (passed in 1954) prohibits churches and other tax-exempt organizations from "directly or indirectly participating in, or intervening in, any political campaign on behalf of (or in opposition to) any candidate for elective public office." President Donald Trump made a campaign promise to "get rid of and totally destroy" it. See https://www.npr.org/2017/02/03/513187940/the-johnson-amendment-in-five-questions-and-answers.
[71] — 2 Timothy 3:5
[72] — Luke 12:32

ESSAY 16

[73] — Frankel, Julia. "Israel's military campaign in Gaza seen as among the most destructive in recent history, experts say." (January 11, 2024.) *apnews.com*. https://apnews.com/article/israel-gaza-bombs-destruction-death-toll-scope-419488c511f83c85baea22458472a796, accessed November 10, 2024.
[74] — "Israel hits Gaza Strip with the equivalent of two nuclear bombs." *euromedmonitor.org*. (November 02, 2023.) https://euromedmonitor.org/en/article/5908/Israel-hits-Gaza-Strip-with-the-equivalent-of-two-nuclear-bombs, accessed November 10, 2024.
[75] — Çalli, Muhammed Enes. "Amount of Israeli bombs dropped on Gaza surpasses that of World War II." *aa.com*. (April 6, 2024). https://www.aa.com.tr/en/middle-east/amount-of-israeli-bombs-dropped-on-gaza-surpasses-that-of-world-war-ii/3239665, accessed November 10, 2024.
[76] — El Deeb, Mohammad Jahjouh. "After a year of Israeli bombardment, Gaza is in ruins. It may take years to rebuild." *pbs.org*. (October 7, 2024.) https://www.pbs.org/newshour/world/after-a-year-of-israeli-bombardment-gaza-is-in-ruins-it-may-take-years-to-rebuild, accessed November 10, 2024. If the current blockade of Gaza is not lifted after the war is over, other estimates suggest rebuilding could take 350 years.
[77] — "UNWRA reports 10 children lose legs every day in Gaza," *LeMonde.fr* (June 25, 2024.) https://www.lemonde.fr/en/international/article/2024/06/25/unrwa-reports-10-children-lose-legs-every-day-in-gaza_6675697_4.html#, accessed November 10, 2024. As of October, the United Nations calls Gaza "home to the argest cohort of child amputees in modern history." See, "UN: Gaza home to largest number of amputee children in modern history," *middleeastmonitor.com*. https://www.middleeastmonitor.com/20241011-un-gaza-home-to-largest-number-of-amputee-children-in-modern-history/.

[78] — Awad, Alex. *Palestinian Memories: The Story of a Palestinian Mother and Her People.* (n.p., 2008), 14.

[79] — Mitri, Raheb. "The Bible and Land Colonization," *Theologies of Land: Contested Land, Spatial Justice, and Identity,* eds. K.K. Yeo and Gene L. Green. (Eugene: Cascade, 2021), 28.

ESSAY 17

[80] — Although abortion was a rallying cry for many years, recent election surveys found the economy, immigration, and other issues as more important than abortion, even among religious voters.

[81] — Nash, Elizabeth and Peter Ephross. "State Policy Trends 2022: In a Devastating Year, US Supreme Court's Decision to Overturn Roe Leads to Bans, Confusion, and Chaos." *Guttmacher.org.* (December 2022.) https://www.guttmacher.org/2022/12/state-policy-trends-2022-devastating-year-us-supreme-courts-decision-overturn-roe-leads, accessed November 14, 2024.

[82] — Released in 1984, *The Silent Scream* was a strong force in the pro-life movement, but received criticism from some in the medical community for drastically enlarging the on-screen size of the fetus, questions whether the stage of fetal development was pain sensitive, and whether fetuses had a concept of danger (in responding to the abortion implements). See links in the "Medical community" section here: https://en.wikipedia.org/wiki/The_Silent_Scream.

[83] — Author's paraphrase of Jeremiah 1:5–10, and 4.

[84] — "Incest Rates in America." *IncestAware.org.* (n.d.) https://www.incestaware.org/incest-rates-in-america-and-beyond, accessed November 14, 2024. All underlines in the quote are hyperlinks in the original online article.

[85] — Humiston, Katelyn. "Rapists and Child Custody: The Battle for Parental Rights in the U.S." *The Justice Journal.* gwjusticejournal.com. (May 11, 2022). https://gwjusticejournal.com/2022/05/11/rapists-and-child-custody-the-battle-for-parental-rights-in-the-u-s/, accessed November 14, 2024.

[86] — Luchetta, Julie. "Women forced out of Idaho for medically-needed abortions sue for clarification on ban." *BoiseStatePublicRadio.org.* (Updated November 14, 2024) https://www.boisestatepublicradio.org/news/2024-11-13/idaho-abortion-hearings-adkins, November 14, 2024.

[87] — Carcopino, Jérôme. *Daily Life in Ancient Rome, Second Edition.* (New Haven: Yale University Press, 2003), 77.

[88] — Black, Edwin. *War on the Weak: Eugenics and America's Campaign to Create a Master Race.* (New York: Four Walls Eight Windows, 2003), xv.

[89] — Ibid, xvi.

About Marty

Marty Duren is a longtime writer, pastor, and public theologian. His interest in the Christian life as a "stranger in a strange land" has taken him to six of the seven continents telling the gospel of Jesus Christ, driven him to pursue justice, and compelled him to write on subjects like the ones contained in The Disparate Ones.

He has bylines at WashingtonPost.com, FactsandTrends.net, ChurchLeaders.com, Baptist Press, Christian Post, Baptist News Global, the Baptist Paper, and others. Marty has freelanced copy for content marketing, ghostwritten three books, as well as editing, proofreading and publishing multiple volumes. You can connect with him on Bluesky, Facebook, and at blog.martyduren.com, where you can subscribe to blog updates for free.

Marty and Sonya have four adult children, three sons-in-law, two grandsons, a rowdy collie named Watson, and a calico cat named Scout, who would require, but not deserve, an essay of her own.

www.ingramcontent.com/pod-product-compliance
Lightning Source LLC
Chambersburg PA
CBHW030952170125
20531CB00041B/540